The
Mindfulness
Toolbox for
Relationships

Self • Family • Lover • Friends • Community • Workplace • World

50 Practical Tips, Tools & Handouts
for Building Compassionate Connections

Donald Altman, MA, LPC
author of the award-winning *The Mindfulness Toolbox*

Praise for The Mindfulness Toolbox for Relationships

"Everyone interested in creating healthier and more rewarding relationships of any kind needs to read *The Mindfulness Toolbox for Relationships*. Therapists who work with individuals or couples will find dozens of wonderful tools and easy-to-use handouts designed to create healthy, caring, and satisfying relationships. Donald Altman's clearly written-mindfulness exercises will have you feeling restored and hopeful about the relationships in your life."

-**Debra Burdick**, LCSW, BCN
Author of *Mindfulness Skills Workbook for Clinicians and Clients*,
Mindfulness Skills for Kids and Teens, and *Mindfulness Skills for Kids Card Deck and Games*

"*The Mindfulness Toolbox for Relationships* is an insightful and practical guide for anyone in a relationship—at work or at home—who wants to make it better. Information is presented in bite-sized nuggets and in a workbook format that makes insights accessible and practical. The real-world, experiential tools will help you to quickly and directly gain an in-depth understanding of yourself and others. I will definitely be using these tips and tools with my coaching and business clients."

-**John Baldoni**, Trust Across America Lifetime Achievement Honoree, internationally recognized executive coach and leadership educator; author of *Lead with Purpose and MOXIE: The Secret to Bold and Gutsy Leadership*

"Mindfulness represents a family of related practices that improve self-regulation, attention, self-inquiry, well-being and psychological health. To that end, Donald Altman's *The Mindfulness Toolbox for Relationships* is an excellent and thoughtful guide that offers a host of practical suggestions to enhance relationships with well-being, depth, and meaning"

-**John Arden**, PhD, ABPP
author of *Mind-Brain-Gene* and *Brain2Brain*

The Mindfulness Toolbox for Relationships © 2018 by Donald Altman

Published by
PESI Publishing & Media
PESI, Inc
3839 White Ave
Eau Claire, WI 54703

Editing: Debra Burdick, Bookmasters
Layout: Bookmasters
Cover: Amy Rubenzer

ISBN: 9781683731269

Proudly printed in the United States

PESI
Publishing
& Media
www.pesipublishing.com

This book is dedicated to peace
and all who seek peace
within and without.

May each grain of mindfulness
be a blessing of awakening
on behalf of all who suffer.

May each grain of mindfulness
be an instrument of peace and love
for the benefit and well-being of all.

About the Author

Donald Altman, M.A., LPC is a psychotherapist, award-winning author, and former Buddhist monk. A featured expert in *The Mindfulness Movie*, he spent several years teaching in Portland State University's Interpersonal Neurology Certificate Program.

Known for pioneering books that teach how to integrate ancient mindfulness into daily life, his award-winning books include: *The Mindfulness Toolbox*—winner of two *Gold IBPA Benjamin Franklin™ Awards* as best book in the "Psychology" and "Body-Mind-Spirit" categories; *Clearing Emotional Clutter*—selected "One of the Best Spiritual Books of 2016;" and *The Mindfulness Code*—chosen "One of the Best Spiritual Books of 2010." Donald served as a board member and past vice-president of The Center for Mindful Eating. Profiled in the Living Spiritual Teacher's project, he is a business and wellness program consultant, keynote speaker, and international mindfulness workshop leader. More info: Mindfulpractices.com

Table of Contents

Section 1 – Essential Mindfulness Relationship Tips for Therapists

The acronym P.A.I.R. U.P. places mindfulness squarely in a relational context. Learn how to describe the key benefits of mindful relationships.

Using a 'mindful model of change' that places the emphasis on the journey, as opposed to the destination, can make one's experience more effective.

Identifying an individual's learning styles is a clue for understanding how that person gets present—whether through sound, sight, or touch. Here you will discover how to engage this aspect of mindfulness for relationships.

Mindfulness is the inside-out intervention for mindful relationships because it helps integrate and rewire the brain for compassion, kindness, and empathy.

Just as treatment plans and goal setting are important tasks for clients, getting connected to one's deepest values changes how one acts in the moment.

Learn how mindful awareness of the body and mirror neurons can transform how clients interact and attune with others in their lives.

Learn how mindfulness creates a fertile ground for reshaping relational experiences and cultivating feelings of safety and security.

Social connections provide a key resource for overcoming loss, moving beyond grief, and turning toward joy.

Explore why mindfulness is a useful tool for getting unstuck from conflicts and toxic patterns.

Discover how an awareness of strengths can transform how anyone views and deals with relationship stress and difficulties.

Section 2 – Mindfulness Tools for Relationship with Self

This tool will help couples and others learn how to honor the learning styles of others, as well as provide new insights for improved communication.

This quick and easy-to-use mindfulness practice is designed to help anyone drop out of the busy mind and settle firmly in the body.

In such a fractured and distracted modern world, the ability to center and regulate emotions with diaphragmatic breath practice becomes essential.

By learning how to constructively distance from negative thoughts, individuals will learn to sit with emotional disruptions instead of reacting to them.

Rather than try to escape the difficulties of life, this meditative practice shows how to face challenging situations with self-acceptance, insight, and openness.

Find out how the Loving-Kindness Meditation warms the heart, as well as overcomes animosity and fear that can do lasting harm to relationships.

Explore body sensations moment-by-moment as a way of "minding the body" and enhancing self-awareness and focus.

Having self-compassion means standing up for yourself. Here's a thoughtful mindfulness approach to getting your needs met.

Developing relational resilience is vital for interpersonal stability and a sense of hope amid the changing landscape of relationships.

When things get chaotic or disruptive, diaphragmatic breathing helps you realign and attune with others, as well as return to a place of equanimity.

Section 3 – Mindfulness Tools for Relationship with Friends, Family & Lovers

Acceptance is a necessary and healing salve for letting go of and letting be those things that can't be controlled in a relationship.

The acronym C.U.R.I.O.U.S. engages a newfound sense of curiosity and fresh eyes when dealing with others—even those difficult persons in one's life.

Life is messy and everyone suffers in some way. This practice shows how compassion can transform even challenging relationships and life situations.

Section 5 – Mindfulness Tools for Relationship with the Natural World

Investigate how the seasons of nature provide a roadmap for understanding the different stages of relationships and when a healthy change is called for.

This hopeful and peaceful practice enhances our sense of interbeing and harmony with those we care about and the planet that supports us.

Acknowledgments

Mindfulness is being spread by many people, and my gratitude goes out to all the mindfulness teachers and students who are helping reduce suffering and increase compassion through their efforts. I want to thank my late teacher, the Venerable U. Silananda, as well as Ashin Thitzana, U. Thondara, and the monks and community of the Burma Buddhist Monastery, Lama Surya Das, and other like-minded teachers, friends, and guides. I am very grateful for the enthusiastic support of my friends, who have always been kind enough to offer their helpful comments and feedback. This book would not be possible without my thoughtful, caring, and creative collaborators at PESI Publishing & Media, including but not limited to publisher Linda Jackson, Hillary Jenness, Karsyn Morse, and the rest of this excellent publishing team. I'm honored to be working with you on books that change lives for the better.

In particular, I want to deeply thank Maria Brignola for her wonderful suggestions, editing ideas, and creative support along the journey of this book from beginning to end. As I've said before, you are my *Bak'u del Cuore*. And to my first creative angel, my mother Barbara, the love, gratitude, and blessings I send to you will never be enough.

Books by
Donald Altman

Introduction

When I was asked to write a follow-up to *The Mindfulness Toolbox*, I was excited to develop new and useful mindfulness tools for both clinicians and individuals. While *The Mindfulness Toolbox* targeted anxiety, depression, stress, and pain, I wanted the new one to be equally beneficial but entirely fresh, practical, and engaging. Keeping that in mind, and after much reflection, the focus for this new book became clear: What better topic to focus on than relationships?

WHO IS THIS BOOK FOR?

If you really want to learn mindfulness, there's no better place to start than in a relational context. That's because everything we do touches relationship. We have a relationship to our inner world of thoughts, the body, and our senses. Then there's the external world of relationships—the complex number of ways that we relate to everything around us—including the people we interact with and the very environment in which we live, breathe, and eat. Any of these relationships can leave us feeling uneasy and unsafe; or, they can leave us feeling solid, stable, and supported. Mindfulness helps navigate the way toward healthier, sustainable relationships.

Simply, this book is for mental health clinicians, as well as individuals/couples or others who want to cultivate better relationships.

At home, work, or anywhere, the practices here can build thoughtful, effective, compassionate, collaborative, understanding, and loving connections.

For therapists who are working with clients, this book will provide you with over 40 unique and detailed mindfulness handouts. Almost all of these handouts can be done individually—even if a handout mentions working with another. Because this is a skills-based book, skills can be either demonstrated (as a guided script) or explored in session, and then put into action.

For individuals, couples, or others getting this book for their own use, it's okay to practice on your own or with another. Either way, you'll be learning how to use mindfulness to relate at a profound level to the vast inner and outer environments of your life.

Mindfulness changes relationships because it engages an unfiltered and childlike sense of curiosity and openness. This helps us escape the "small view" of the ego, the "I," "me," "my," and "mine." This means that even that "difficult person" in your life can be experienced in a new way. Of course, escaping the gravitational pull of one's personal history and a strongly cemented egocentric perspective is not an easy task. But even small steps can bring a sense of liberation and freedom from old, stuck habits and toxic ways of reacting to any of these relationships.

With these concepts in mind, *The Mindfulness Toolbox for Relationships* was designed to provide practical tools for addressing many issues that impact daily living and the stresses that face us in the real world. Relationships can serve as the one constant to buffer us against difficult transition and change. For example, several different studies have correlated a positive relationship with greater health and happiness. By inviting in greater awareness, compassion, and openness, mindfulness skillfully gives us the means for uplifting and inspiring ourselves, as well as others.

This is especially true for those of us living in the 21st century, considering the new challenges facing relationships that have never existed in the past. While our ability to communicate and stay in touch with a wider social network is unparalleled, living in an always on 24 hours/7 days a week instant-gratification world can get in the way of the slower *face-to-face human means of wiring our brains*, as has occurred for millennia. There's also the question of how technology may be rewiring our brains and muting the brain's innately wired ability to experience empathy and recognize facial emotions. The prevalence of technology and social media has grown to such an extent that the APA's Stress in America™ Survey now addresses the role of technology and social media in producing stress.[1]

The study even identified "constant checkers"—people who constantly looked at their email accounts, cell phone texts, and social media accounts. These individuals experienced significantly higher stress levels than those who didn't have this checking behavior. In fact, 43 percent of Americans were found to be constant checkers! Studies like this are great, but sometimes all we have to do is look around and ask a simple question:

How has technology changed the interactions with others in my life or household?

It's not technology per se, but *how* we use it that matters. Bringing mindfulness into our relationships may help everything else fall into place more naturally, including healthy technology boundaries. To that end, *The Mindfulness Toolbox for Relationships* offers accessible tools for creating stable and safe relationships that will act as a touchstone to steady us against the currents of rapid change and transition that can leave us reeling, spinning, and reactive.

You can think of the tools in this book as human awareness technology for living well with others and ourselves.

ROADMAP TO USING THIS BOOK AND ITS FOUR KEY FEATURES

To make the book easy to follow, it's divided into five sections that are structured much like the original *The Mindfulness Toolbox*. Mindfulness has always been about directly facing and confronting the difficulties that one must endure. But *how* these are embraced makes all the difference. For that reason, the strategies, tips, and handouts in this book take a positive slant.

Let's briefly look at four unique features that are built into *The Mindfulness Toolbox for Relationships*. Firstly, there's **Section 1 – *Essential Mindful Relationship Tips for Therapists*, which provides general tips and ideas for making your treatment more effective.** This section offers foundational material for using and deepening your understanding of the tools in the book. These tips are designed to help the user—whether a clinician and/or individual—be more creative and adaptable in applying the tools. There may be times, for example, when you want to deepen a discussion about relational brain science or how intentionality helps rewire the brain. Basic concepts such as tips for making relational mindfulness effective and working with the body are also explored here.

The second feature is an exploration of mindful learning styles. Tip #3, *Identifying and Implementing Mindful Learning Styles* offers valuable ideas for matching the right tools with clients. It's based on the following idea:

How someone learns is also how that person gets mindful and in the present moment.

---

[1] https://www.apa.org/news/press/releases/stress/2017/technology-social-media.PDF (accessed September, 2017).

This is of no small consequence, because when you identify a client's learning style you can more quickly, easily, and accurately identify which of the tools in the book will fit with that individual. Clients will appreciate this too, because gaining an awareness of how another person gets mindful allows for greater understanding and patience for others. To make this accessible, each tool will list upfront which mindful learning styles it accesses.

The third special feature included in these pages is the detailed handouts. These are clearly written as *readable scripts*, and in some cases *guided meditations*, that you can use to demonstrate any practice in the course of a therapy session. Directly guiding clients, and then giving them the handout for reference to use at home is an effective way of helping them learn and process. For those who prefer listening and being guided through practices, the scripts offer the option of making it easy to record these, or even modify them if that works best.

Lastly, the fourth unique feature in *The Mindfulness Toolbox for Relationships* is the ability to quickly bundle, or customize, a set of related practices. Cross-referencing of related practices lets you easily customize a set of tools for clients without having to laboriously figure out which ones fit together. For example, practices for developing forgiveness, compassion, and acceptance will be bundled together for persons needing those strategies or who want to deepen their understanding of those areas.

Because this book is a toolbox, it's designed so that you can choose the best tool for the job. That means you can jump directly to any practice that addresses a need. However, it may be helpful to first look through the Section 1 readings as a way to prepare for using the tools most effectively.

Section 2 – *Mindful Tools for Relationship with Self* provides several important methods for self-regulating, tapping personal values, and expanding awareness of mind-body-spirit. These are essential practices and a starting point for well-being and clarity. While this section is not intended as a mindfulness program, these tools offer an initial training for those who might want to move on to mindfulness retreats or further training.

Keep in mind that for many persons, working with Section 2 will be an important mindfulness skill-building experience. It's not that someone with no prior mindfulness experience can't use the tools in other sections; rather, this section provides basic tools for self-regulation and self-awareness—which is much like teaching someone how to swim while wearing a life preserver. It can make the process easier in the long run once the basics concepts are understood. Depending on the issue, one or two tools from Section 1 might be all that's needed before moving on to other tools in the rest of the book. This approach also lets you start in small steps, which builds efficacy and primes anyone for greater success later on.

Section 3 – *Mindfulness Tools for Relationship with Friends, Family & Lovers* provides tools designed to reduce reactivity and improve fractured relationships. As such, this section introduces important practices for forgiveness, acceptance, respect, and compassion, as well as mindful rituals for transitioning.

Section 4 – *Mindfulness Tools for Relationship with Community, Workplace & World* expands the reach of mindfulness by offering tools for transforming how we experience and interact with others out in the world. Here, practices include such things as inclusiveness, the power of giving, establishing mindful boundaries, and more.

Section 5 – *Mindful Tools for Relationship with the Natural World* takes us full circle by acknowledging the wisdom and lessons that nature has to offer. The practices and tools in this section can be used to help anyone restore depleted mental energy, find hope, release one's worries, and find new hope through loving-kindness.

Taking the Journey

Mindfulness is not a final answer, but a day-to-day, moment-to-moment journey of peace and awakening. It is a gentle approach to change that addresses and acknowledges and embraces the richness of being human, in all its complexity. This is an exciting time to be alive, and mindfulness offers a time-tested means of facing life and reducing harm—in all of our relationships.

Mindfulness is the ultimate human awareness technology. It shines the laser-like light of awareness on all that we do. It doesn't point the finger at others, but rather, nudges us to appreciate and carefully use the precious gift of consciousness and attention. What are we drawn to? What are we repelled by? How are these attachments affecting others and ourselves? Mindfulness is not about detaching from life, but participating fully, in a meaningful and hopeful way. In a world where it's all too easy to see our world and relationships through the lens of duality and absolutes, such as good and bad, or black and white, the practices here offer another way.

As you and others prepare to step on the mindful relationship path, let me share the words of the Buddha as written in the Dhammapada:[2]

> *Animosity does not eradicate animosity.*
> *Only by loving-kindness is animosity dissolved.*
> *This law is ancient and eternal.*

It is my hope that this book contributes to bringing more wellness and balance into the lives of those you are interacting with. May we all continue the journey of reducing suffering and changing lives for the better through relationships—a true journey to the heart.

---

[2] Ananda Maitreya, translator, *The Dhammapada* (Berkeley, CA: Parallax Press, 1995), p. 2.

Essential Mindful Relationship Tips for Therapists

Tip #1	# P.A.I.R. U.P. for Mindful Relationships

THOUGHTS FOR THERAPISTS

What does it mean to have a "mindful relationship"? Why is this important? These are vital questions and essential topics to cover when introducing relational mindfulness to clients. Simply an exploration and discussion about mindfulness itself can help someone understand why relationships can benefit from using mindfulness. That's because mindfulness already encompasses the idea of relationship. If you are being mindful, you are naturally in a more aware relationship to whatever is occurring—be it internally through sensations and feelings in the body, thoughts and emotions experienced in the mind, or externally by what is happening in your life.

At its core, mindfulness dissolves the illusion of separateness that we believe exists. In doing so, it cultivates what I call the *We-Thou awareness*. Martin Buber referred to this as *I-Thou*, while Vietnamese monk Thich Nhat Hanh has called this *interbeing*. Whatever the terminology, mindfulness loosens the grip of the egocentric viewpoint. As a result, it softens those who use it; it lets us expand in empathy and compassion, in trust and acceptance.

One tool I've developed for understanding what mindfulness is and how it works is the acronym P.A.I.R. U.P., which was first described in my book *Clearing Emotional Clutter*. This explanation paints a broader picture of mindfulness and how it naturally draws us into the world of relationships. When relationships aren't going smoothly we need to learn how to *pair up*, or be a better fit with whatever is occurring in our relationships and life situation. This acronym is not intended as a final, most comprehensive definition, and there are many diverse and wonderful ways of describing mindfulness— from the Buddha's traditional *Satipatthana sutta* (*The Foundations of Mindfulness*) to descriptions of it in various programs.

TIPS FOR INTRODUCING MINDFULNESS TO CLIENTS

Here are potential points to share as you introduce mindful relationships.

✓ Mindfulness methods have been used for many years for such things as stress reduction, reducing anxiety, depression, and even chronic pain.

✓ A program called Mindfulness-Based Relationship Enhancement showed how mindful relationships produced many benefits, including greater acceptance, closeness, and higher levels of relationship satisfaction and happiness.[3]

✓ Mindfulness is a set of learned skills that anyone can learn.

✓ Mindfulness has been shown to change the brain from the inside out.

---

[3] James Carson, Kimberly Carson, et al.; Mindfulness-based relationship enhancement, *Behavior Therapy*, Volume 35, Issue 3, Summer 2004, pp. 471-494. http://doi.org/10.1016/S0005-7894(04)80028-5

✓ It's advisable to discuss the P.A.I.R. U.P. acronym in person before offering the handout. This way the client can take the handout for review, as well as spend some time reflecting on it before returning to process it.

✓ Optionally, you may want to explore some words that describe mindfulness in a way that fits best with each person. (A complete list is in the *Expanding the Mindfulness Vocabulary* chapter in *The Mindfulness Toolbox*.) Here are a few examples of ways to describe mindfulness:

- opening to the moment
- noticing the truth of change
- an open-hearted acceptance of this moment
- living in the *what-is* as opposed to the *what-if*
- getting freed from habit and reactivity
- acceptance and letting-go
- focusing on the moment
- changing the history channel
- loving awareness
- tuning in to others
- moment-to-moment awareness of the breath
- stop, look, and listen
- non-dual awareness
- unplugging
- finding the center
- prayerfulness
- leaving the busy mind by dropping into the body
- awareness that doesn't take sides
- inner hospitality
- cultivating a neutral, detached awareness
- getting in the zone
- hitting the pause button
- impartial witness/spectator
- making friends with your mind
- non-blaming; openness
- picturing the ocean or a river
- creating space (from negativity)

Learn How to P.A.I.R. U.P. with Mindfulness

Instructions

Think of the following acronym P.A.I.R. U.P. as one way you can bring mindfulness in your life. Mindfulness doesn't mean things are going to be perfect; it accepts that sometimes things can get messy. But even then, you can *pair up* with these skills to find balance and a new perspective. Read and then answer the questions.

P — *Present-Moment Participation*

When you whole-heartedly participate and engage with others, you build trust and make stronger connections and friendships.

A — *Attuned Acceptance*

While you might not be able to control what happens in life, you can control your attitude. Cultivating acceptance offers greater calm; attunement means you can have empathy and a deeper understanding for others, even if they don't happen to agree with you. These are both keys to finding harmony with others.

I — *Intentionality*

When you consciously choose how to act and speak each day, you invite a heart-centered approach to all relationships—whether at home or at work.

R — *Reflection*

When you pause to reflect and investigate your relationships—as well as think about what values matter most deeply to you—you can get unstuck from old patterns, discover fresh insights, and move in new directions.

U — *Understanding of Suffering*

When you realize that all persons suffer in some way, you gain a greater sense of patience and compassion for others.

P — *Purposeful Partnership*

What if others supported your dreams, and vice versa? By finding your purpose and supporting others, you help grow a web of meaningful community partnership.

Reflections

Which one of the skills would make a positive difference in your life right now, and why?

_____

_____

_____

_____

_____

Which skill feels most challenging to you, and why?

_____

_____

_____

_____

_____

Which of the skills do you currently use in your life and relationships?

_____

_____

_____

_____

_____

What would most change in your life if you could bring P.A.I.R. U.P. into it?

_____

_____

_____

_____

_____

Tip #2 | # Managing Expectations with a Mindful Model of Change

THOUGHTS FOR THERAPISTS

For good or bad, expectations matter. Part of the job of those working in the health care field is to manage those expectations, especially when people want quick fixes. Because we live in a world and culture that is more and more steeped in what can be viewed as a fix-it quickly expectation that I call the *Mechanical-Replacement Model of Change*, it's not surprising that people want a quick fix when it comes to emotional wellness and relationships.

A perfect example of this mechanical model of change is when your car needs repair. For example, if your car's battery is dead, it is immediately swapped out with a new and fully functional battery. This method of change is quick, fast, and effective. Certainly, there are advantages for this rapid replacement method.

- Useful with independent systems allowing for replacement.
- Predictable or measurable in how long the procedure/process will take.
- Using new and perfect replacement parts means fewer future problems.
- Shortened need for follow-up and monitoring.

Humans, however, are not machines. So before you feel like you need to learn an entire set of mental and emotional replacement skills to get people "fixed" and out the door right away, take a nice long breath! The primary disadvantage of the mechanical model of change is that emotions cannot simply be replaced. In fact, viewing oneself in a mechanical way is likely to cause increased frustration and impatience. When you are feeling sad, angry, or grief-stricken, can you really expect to get a three-year warranty on your feelings? How can you replace that part of the brain that processes emotions and trauma? Now, while there may be times when a mechanical model works—such as when replacing a hip or using a pacemaker for irregular heartbeat—we need to accept that the human mind-body is more complex than any machine.

A one-size-fits-all mechanical model cannot account for the fact that humans are amazingly unique. For instance, the human brain alone contains over 100 billion neurons with trillions of connections—a number greater than all the stars in the universe. That means that each human who you meet today is the most unique human in the entire universe—yourself included! This is a powerful idea that later on will be employed to help those in a relationship to deeply understand the preciousness of the person(s) with whom they are connecting.

TIPS FOR WORKING WITH CLIENTS

- ✓ Before using the following handout, address a client's change expectations.
- ✓ Discuss the mechanical-replacement model and the Mindful Acceptance and Commitment model of change (described on the following handout).
- ✓ Describe how the mindful model is a more gentle approach that allows one to embrace change with a greater sense of peace, patience, acceptance, and willingness.

The Mindful Acceptance and Commitment Model of Change

How you view change can have an impact on whether or not you fully embrace it. This handout will introduce you to a mindfulness-oriented model of change that draws upon your uniqueness. Essentially, this model states that change begins by accepting your present condition, while at the same time committing to learning new skills that can actually rewire the neural network in your brain.

How It Works

- Change starts with acceptance—rather than avoidance—of what is happening in your life right now that you want to change; also, this means accepting that stress increases a tendency to return to old habits.
- Change is collaborative and happens through relationship and experience.
- Success is defined as experiencing the process; it values learning from mistakes and accepts this as an important part of the process.
- Change requires a commitment to learning and practicing mindfulness-based skills over time.
- Change doesn't happen all at once, and the focus is on the day-by-day process rather than on some future outcome.

Advantages of this Method

- Useful for complex, holistic human systems.
- A non-blaming, accepting, forgiving, and gentle style of change.
- Helps you understand the effects of stress on your behavior and life.
- Gives you the skills needed to create reliable change and prepare for learning from mistakes.
- Good for tracking and monitoring complexity.

As useful as the Acceptance-Commitment-Skill perspective is, it presents some special challenges. For example, it takes time and effort and requires patience. It may not be as fast as the mechanical-replacement change model, which could cause frustration or disappointment.

In the space below, write down what you think are the challenges you will face in using this model of change:

_____

_____

_____

In what area(s) of your life do you think this style of change might be useful?

_____

_____

_____

Name one way in which this model of change might make things easier for you or others.

_____

_____

_____

Tip #3 | Identifying and Implementing Mindful Learning Styles

THOUGHTS FOR THERAPISTS

While learning styles were also featured in *The Mindfulness Toolbox*, they take on greater depth and dimension in these pages. Integrating mindfulness and learning styles is an important way to utilize mindfulness interventions. This is a novel way of adapting and applying mindfulness, one that I teach in my workshops. Using this method, you will collaborate with clients in fashioning tailored interventions that access someone's natural style for getting highly attentive, focused, and present—be it visual, auditory, interpersonal, tactile, or so on. Best of all, I've helped people in relationships recognize not just their *own* style of getting present, but the *styles of those around them*. This can be a discovery for many, and a building block for creating stronger relationships and connecting in newfound ways.

One example of this comes from the time I worked with a couple—let's call them Ron and Cynthia (all names and details are changed)—who had real trouble communicating. It became clear early on that Ron, who loved to play with words and do word puzzles, got very present through the verbal-linguistic learning style. His partner Cynthia, however, loved working with her hands—such as in the garden tending plants or by preparing and cooking food. After they had an argument, Ron would often apologize verbally using his own, natural mindful learning style. But it bothered him that Cynthia would not "say" she was sorry. Instead, she would often prepare a special meal or dish for Ron. His partner's offering did not provide a satisfying sense of closure—until he learned that his partner's language was not words, but was expressed through the body-spatial-tactile way of getting present. After learning his partner's style, Ron learned to wholeheartedly accept his partner's apology, even though it was offered in a different form.

When people in a relationship have vastly different mindful styles, it's vital to know that. Attempting to communicate using mixed styles is akin to shouting at a deaf person or using sign language with someone who has no sight. The message simply isn't going to be effective. Fortunately, by developing a relational awareness of learning styles, anyone can learn to adapt their style to fit what works with others.

To make this concept easy to apply, the beginning of each tool features a list of mindful learning styles that fit best with that particular mindfulness tool. Keep in mind that everyone gets naturally present in more than one way. And since there are nine different mindful learning styles, there are mindfulness tools that can be adapted to fit and work well for a vast range of people.

TIPS FOR USING MINDFUL LEARNING STYLES WITH CLIENTS

When you find a particular practice isn't engaging for a client, you may want to explore learning styles in more detail. Here are some useful resources.

- ✓ The book *7 Kinds of Smart: Identifying and Developing Your Multiple Intelligences* by Thomas Armstrong actually includes nine learning styles in all.
  - Use the quick assessments in this book with individuals, couples, or groups in order to help identify learning styles. This can be done in session or as homework.

✓ Another resource is my own book, *The Joy Compass*, which devotes an entire chapter to matching mindfulness and contemplative practices with the various learning styles.

✓ Here are two useful online resources that will score and determine learning styles in a matter of minutes.

- Edutopia, the brainchild of filmmaker George Lucas, features a *Multiple Intelligences Self-Assessment* that consists of 24 questions and can be completed in only five minutes. This assessment offers a top tier of learning styles.
    - Visit: https://www.edutopia.org/multiple-intelligences-assessment
- The *Rogers Indicator of Multiple Intelligences* provides a 56-question assessment that is scored online, and it features two tiers of learning styles. In other words, the primary ways that one gets present, in addition to secondary modes of getting present.
    - Visit: http://www.personal.psu.edu/bxb11/MI/rimi2.htm

✓ After using these resources, have clients put together a list of their primary mindful learning styles. Also, have them list examples of how their passions and hobbies express those styles. You might also consider asking the following questions to reveal mindful learning styles:

- "What would your most fun day look like? What would you be doing?"
- "What would your partner's (or others) most fun day look like? What would your partner be doing?"

Here is a list of the nine intelligences, or learning styles:

1. Verbal-Linguistic
2. Visual-Spatial
3. Sound-Musical
4. Bodily-Kinesthetic-Tactile
5. Mathematical-Science-Logical
6. Social-Interpersonal
7. Reflective-Intrapersonal
8. Natural World
9. Existential-Meaning

CONCLUSIONS

You can become a "learning style detective" and figure out how someone uses attention to get in the present moment by asking some simple questions. For example, asking what hobbies or activities an individual enjoys—both now and historically—can give you strong clues as to that individual's present-awareness style. Those who like going to the beach, for example, may be more visual, nature-oriented, and intrapersonal oriented. Of course the deeper you go with the questions, the more clearly you'll be able to identify mindful learning styles. Another good question is to inquire about someone's last vacation: Where did they go? What did they do? How did this activity make them feel?

This information can be easily obtained as part of an initial intake and filed away for later use. If clients have problems staying with a particular mindfulness practice, consider investigating learning styles using one of the assessment tools mentioned above. Integrating mindful learning styles into relationship work is a powerful and creative way to work with anyone, as well as using this in your own life. Have fun with it!

Tip #4 | Integrating the Relational Brain

THOUGHTS FOR THERAPISTS

In his Message for a New Millennium, the Dalai Lama wrote, "Human problems will, of course, always remain—but the way to resolve them should be through dialogue and discussion. The next century should be a century of dialogue and discussion rather than one of war and bloodshed."[4]

Naturally, one of the impediments to communication is that of expanding beyond the limiting egocentric point of view that we all possess. The Dalai Lama refers to "internal disarmament" as a way of overcoming negativity and fear. Letting go of the small "I-centered" viewpoint and disarming ourselves of negativity is no easy task. Consider that it takes six months of daily work to train a wild horse until the trainer can place the bit in the horse's mouth. The human mind is infinitely more untamed, willful, and wild.

Fortunately, the human brain is wired for connection and communication. The prefrontal cortex, which is located behind the eyebrow ridge and the underside front of the brain, does a lot of its initial wiring in the first 10-24 months as we communicate face-to-face with our caregivers. The new field of interpersonal neurobiology, or IPNB, shows us that even if there are compromises in how this occurs, this prefrontal area of the brain can still rewire and change to produce feelings of connection, safety, and trust. Interpersonal neurobiology is steeped in using mindfulness, and it focuses on understanding how the brain is highly relational and experiential. I like to describe IPNB through the three 'R's:

- The brain is **Relational**.
    - We learn through empathy and connecting with others.
- The brain is **Reflective**.
    - We learn and gain insight from reflecting inwardly and looking within.
- The brain is **Regulatory**.
    - We can pause and decide on a course of action by responding instead of just impulsively reacting.

In fact, 21st-century neuroscience affirms that we possess these mindfulness abilities. Amazingly, there is a built-in system of specialized neurons located in the brain's frontal lobe—called mirror neurons—that links us to others. Neuroscientist Vilayanur Ramachandran described this when he said, "It's as though this neuron is adopting the other person's point of view, and it's almost as if it's performing a virtual reality simulation of the other person's action."[5] These neurons can assist in learning complex social behaviors as well as allow for empathy—again, that unique ability to take another's point of view. No wonder that Ramachandran refers to these as "Gandhi neurons," or "empathy neurons"!

It's important to know that this relation-ability does not in any way mean tossing out the individual self. However, mindfulness practices inevitably get clients out of themselves and closer to a sense of

---

[4] "Message for the New Millennium," https://www.dalailama.com/messages/world-peace/millennium-message (accessed April 2017).

[5] "The neurons that shaped civilization," https://www.ted.com/talks/vs_ramachandran_the_neurons_that_shaped_civilization#t-230139 (accessed April 2017).

connectedness between all living things. As mentioned in Tip #1, this shift in awareness from *I* to *We* promotes a compassionate viewpoint and the understanding that all persons have suffered in some way. After all, don't humans—indeed, all living beings—seek to feel safe, healthy, peaceful, and secure?

TIPS FOR WORKING WITH CLIENTS

When working with clients to cultivate *We-Thou* awareness, it can be helpful to first explore the following questions and ideas. (These questions are also included as a part of the handout that follows):

- ✓ How do you know when you are defending your inner sense of self, or ego?
- ✓ At those times, how does defending help or hinder how you connect with others?
- ✓ Was there a time when you felt that someone really understood you?
- ✓ What would be an advantage to truly seeing and experiencing things from another individual's point of view?
- ✓ Is there anything that concerns you about letting go of your own point of view and experiencing what another person is feeling?
- ✓ When using any of these mindfulness practices, you can always return to your own personal point of view at any time.

Cultivating We-Thou Awareness

You might be amazed to know that 21st-century neuroscience affirms that each of us possesses a built-in system of specialized neurons located in the brain's frontal lobe—called mirror neurons—that links us to others. When you think about it, much suffering is caused by viewing things personally. Yes, it's easy to take things personally, but think for a moment how things might be different if you let go of the "I" perspective and experienced things through a "We" perspective.

What follows is just an exploration to see what a "We" perspective would feel like. To make that connection with others in a broader way, ask yourself the following questions. (And in case you're wondering: The "I" is always there, and you can always return to that perspective anytime you want to.)

Reflections

How do you know when you are defending your inner sense of self, or ego? At such times, how does defending help or hinder how you connect with others?

_____

_____

_____

Do you remember a time when you felt that someone really understood you? What did that feel like, and how do you think they were able to see things from your point of view?

_____

_____

_____

What would be an advantage to truly seeing and experiencing things from another individual's point of view?

_____

_____

_____

Is there anything that concerns you about letting go of your own point of view and experiencing what another person is feeling? As mentioned above, you can always return to your own personal point of view at any time.

_____

_____

_____

Tip #5 | Connecting to What Matters

THOUGHTS FOR THERAPISTS

One key aspect of mindfulness that can get overlooked is the importance of one's ethics and values. If mindfulness were *only* about being present and more efficient, and lacked an ethical anchor, one might just become a more aware and effective criminal!

Maybe that's why one of the four foundations of traditional mindfulness focuses on reducing harm by developing one's ethics and morality (the other foundations include awareness of the senses and the body, awareness of thoughts and consciousness, and awareness of feeling and emotions). Some mindfulness programs, such as Acceptance and Commitment Therapy, or ACT, make this a centerpiece of one's work and practice.

Basically, putting one's ethics in the forefront means that when you speak or act, you do so with an awareness of the consequences of that action both on yourself and others. Is your action beneficial? Does is serve in a helpful way? Or, is it self-serving and harmful? Is it driven by personal, selfish needs? Are your actions congruent and in alignment with your deeper values?

To connect with what matters takes thoughtfulness, self-reflection, and time. It means having a commitment to look at the bigger picture of life instead of momentary cravings and desires. Further, it takes a compassionate view that others matter as much as meeting our own needs.

While therapists do a lot of goal setting in treatment planning, it can be just as useful an exercise to do *value-setting* or *ethics-setting*. Often, I use the metaphor of one's values being like the steering wheel in your car. If your car happens to go off the road and onto the shoulder (hey, it happens!), it is by connecting to your deeper intentions and values that you can steer yourself back in the right direction.

We now know, in fact, that the brain is a quantum environment that utilizes intentionality. There are ion channels in each neuron, and when these build up enough of a charge, they cause the neuron to fire. But what is it that produces the ion potential? In *You Are Not Your Brain*, authors Jeffrey Schwartz and Rebecca Gladding examine the power of intentionality to change habits—even deeply entrenched behaviors like Obsessive Compulsive Disorder—and describe the link between one's intentionality and neuronal firing.[6] And, each time that a neuron fires, it subtly shapes a new neural pathway—and that changes how we will think and behave in the future. In this sense, our brains are the result of a lifetime of millions of intentions!

Establishing personal intentions and values for relationships can take many forms. Someone can craft a values statement for one's parenting, friendship, marriage, work relationships, or any other kind of partnership. Focusing on relationship intentions helps clients connect to what matters most in their lives. Most importantly, it's an evolving touchstone that can support them in achieving and maintaining both personal well-being and healthy, sustainable relationships.

---

[6] Jeffrey Schwartz and Rebecca Gladding, *You Are Not Your Brain* (New York: Avery, 2011).

TIPS FOR WORKING WITH CLIENTS

✓ Tool #25, *Using Affirmations as a Relationship GPS*, includes a handout for having clients create an "affirmation statement" that focuses the relationship in a positive direction.

✓ Intentionality naturally brings awareness to those situations where someone has been on autopilot. The benefit of this is that change can only come after there is awareness.

✓ Help clients understand that intentionality also means free will. It means that one can break free of automatic habits and make beneficial choices that matter.

✓ While values deal with the big life issues, *how* these happen is through the little intentional actions that one takes daily. For example:

- The value of "Treating My Partner with Respect," for instance, requires many specific and intentional daily actions such as speaking kindly, listening without interrupting, displaying an unthreatening body language, and engaging in a positive way when coming home or leaving the house. All these and many other interactions can be done with a sense of purpose and meaning.

| Tip #6 | # Working with the Body and Interpersonal Attunement |

THOUGHTS FOR THERAPISTS

Travel back in time 5,000 years to the ancient practices of Tai Chi and Qigong, and you'll discover they worked with what were known as the "three regulations." The first regulation is that of the body, followed by regulation of the breath, and regulation of the mind. These are also essential to mindfulness, and for that reason comprise the three practices, Tools #12, #13, and #14, found in Section 2, *Mindfulness Tools for Relationship with Self.* In their totality, these three form a complete Mindfulness Body/Breath/Mind Meditation.

But why is the body addressed first? Why is it accorded such primacy?

It was early in the twentieth century that Freud wrote, "The ego is first and foremost a bodily ego."[7] Not only is our identity intimately formed and mediated through our body's outer form and sensations, but long before speech and cognition get developed, it is through the body that we communicate and get our needs met. Despite that, it's all too easy to disconnect from the body and get stuck up in the head, with all of its mental workings and contortions. Author James Joyce recognized this disconnect when humorously referring to Mr. Duffy, one of the characters in his novel *Dubliners*:[8]

> *He lived a little distance from his body, regarding his own acts with doubtful side-glances.*

And yet, it's understandable how the body can become an unwelcome home for those experiencing trauma, pain, and anxiety—a home with the doors securely locked and the lights turned off.

Since touch and the body form a vital communication conduit, it's important to recognize the level of a client's embodiment. The field of cognitive science is now exploring *embodied cognition*, or *cognitive embodiment*. This means that the body can affect our mental states, just as our mental states can affect how the body moves and feels. For example, a depressed individual often moves slowly, with a downward gaze; a sad person may have a frowning facial expression. In the same way, changing one's body movement and expression can produce dramatic changes in how that person thinks, acts, and feels.

One group of researchers decided to investigate this idea by working with facial expressions. They found persons with diagnosable depression who were willing to have a Botox treatment that would freeze the frowning muscles in their faces so they couldn't frown. As published in the *Journal for Psychiatric Research*,[9] depressive symptoms, such as sadness, rumination, and anger, quickly went into remission. Essentially, those individuals could no longer make the facial expressions that accompanied the conceptualization of negative thoughts.

---

[7] Sigmund Freud, *The Ego and the Id.* In *Standard Edition of the Complete Psychological Works of Sigmund Freud* (Hogarth: London, UK, 1923), volume 19, p. 26.
[8] James Joyce, *Dubliners* (New York: Oxford University Press, 2008), p. 83.
[9] Wolmer, de Boer, et al., Facing depression with botulinum toxin: a randomized controlled trial, *J Psychiatr Res.* 2012 May; 46(5): 574–81. doi: 10.1016/j.jpsychires.2012.01.027. (accessed April 2017).

The concept of cognitive embodiment has long been embraced in the Dance Movement Therapy field, which for years has developed detailed theories about this. Likewise, mindfulness is steeped in the practice of "dropping into the body" and bringing awareness to how the body affects and regulates mood and thoughts. It's good to know that this concept is gaining a foothold in the cognitive field as well.

TIPS FOR WORKING WITH CLIENTS

✓ If a patient is obviously dissociated from the body, you'll want to go very slowly and always get permission when doing any of the body-oriented practices here.

✓ One of the benefits of dropping into the body is that it tends to pull the plug on the brain's default mode of spinning stories. Let clients know that these practices can be helpful for calming down an anxious or overactive mind.

✓ Let individuals know that the process of becoming more familiar with the body can produce a greater sense of ease and self-acceptance.

- *The Mindfulness Toolbox for Relationships* contains a variety of body-related and relationship connecting practices. Here are some key tools for bringing the body into play:
  - Tool #12, *Body Regulation for Grounding and Attention*
  - Tool #17, *Sensing and Honoring the Body*
  - Tool #20, *Self-Soothing and Synchronized Breathing*
  - Tool #26, *Enhance Relationships with a Positive Shared Memory*
  - Tool #28, *The Tenderness of Touch and Intimacy*
  - Tool #40, *Spontaneous Play*

Tip #7 | # Working with Difficult Relational Histories

THOUGHTS FOR THERAPISTS

One of the questions I often like to pose at my workshops is this: "Does anyone here have a difficult person in your life?" Not surprisingly, most of the hands shoot up. When you stop to consider, who hasn't experienced some kind of difficult relational history? The world is strewn with wounded children, spouses, friendships, and families. From a mindfulness point of view, our history can be honored, but ultimately that background does not need to define or unnecessarily limit our present-moment choices and life experience.

Since mindfulness is about directly confronting what is in your life, this also means not running away from relationships that may be difficult or challenging. I learned this firsthand through the difficult relationship I had with my father. Almost like a master magician's trick, the patterns that had developed in my father-son relationship inevitably popped up elsewhere. It wasn't until I faced this truth and looked more deeply at the roots of my suffering that I was able to make positive changes in the relationship with my father and others.

This is where two important mindfulness concepts come into the picture. The first is the power of acceptance. As described earlier in Tip #1, *P.A.I.R. U.P. for Mindful Relationships*, acceptance is an attitude, a life preserver of sorts. This is not about resigning oneself to a situation or giving up. Rather, acceptance offers the possibility of deciding how to best respond even when confronted with any "impossible" situation—such as an illness. Additional benefits of cultivating acceptance will be examined in more depth in Tool #21, *The Power of Acceptance and Patience*.

The second mindfulness concept that bears mentioning here is that of compassion. As described more in Tool #23, *Grow Your Compassion Container*, the word compassion means, "to be with suffering." With compassion, we are able to navigate difficult histories with more skill and hope. Introducing the ideas of facing one's history, using acceptance, and cultivating compassion can help set the table for using the tools in these pages.

TIPS FOR WORKING WITH CLIENTS

✓ If acceptance and compassion would help, explore these concepts and the various meanings and benefits of these practices.

✓ How have acceptance and compassion helped in other areas of one's life or relationships?

✓ For those harboring old hurts, consider bundling the acceptance and compassion practices mentioned above, Tools #21 and #23, along with Tool #35, *The Gift of Forgiveness*.

  • While some may not warm up to the idea of forgiveness, compassion and acceptance can often open the door through which anyone can become more vulnerable, curious, and willing to explore the idea.

Tip #8 | Working with Loss and Grief

THOUGHTS FOR THERAPISTS

Being in a relationship also means losing a relationship. Somewhere along the line, relationships will conclude. One or the other of a partnership will change, move in a new direction, or decide to leave—sometimes through death. This does not have to be crushing when viewed through one of the main tenets of mindfulness—the concept of impermanence. The Sanskrit word *sampajañña*, which is sometimes translated as clear knowing or clear comprehension, means having an understanding of the nature of impermanence.

No one, for example, stands in the same river of moods or thoughts for very long. Try it. In fact, research has shown that our minds wander an average of nearly 50% of the time. (So, if your mind has wandered while reading this page, I won't take it personally.) Look around, and you'll find that other things are changing and impermanent as well. Being from Chicago, I remember how lustrous and shiny a new car was until it went through the Chicago winter. Eventually, the finish dulled and got nicked from stones and debris. Not to mention that if you drive a car long enough the tires will go bald, and sometimes it happens to the driver (me)!

Even bodily sensations, some of which seem persistent, are less solid and substantial than they may appear. Tool #17, *Sensing and Honoring the Body*, helps to affirm that. All this is not to say that we shouldn't experience our grief and sadness. By all means that's an important process to go through as a normal and necessary response to loss. But developing an understanding of impermanence can help act as a buffer. Sometimes we can benefit from help and support to move forward, and Tool #30, *Imagine Your Joyful Next Chapter*, is designed to help people locate new hope and joy as they step into the unknown.

TIPS FOR WORKING WITH CLIENTS

- ✓ Self-care is sometimes neglected when individuals deal with loss and grief.
- ✓ Mindful self-care means that sleep, exercise, and proper nutrition are being attended to. Without these, it can be difficult to regulate mood and cognition.
- ✓ Relationship loss is a major life stress, so consider bundling together Tool #37, *Softening with G.L.A.D.*, Tool #34, *Spread One Kindness Today*, and the soothing nature practice Tool #41, *Forest Bathing Meditation*.

Tip #9	# Resolving Conflicts

THOUGHTS FOR THERAPISTS

While conflicts are inevitable, there are some very effective mindfulness approaches for harnessing non-reactivity and respect. These are human relationship tools for healing even deep chasms of misunderstanding. But to do so requires a quality of openness and inner reflection that takes commitment, effort, and time. Applying simplistic and predetermined biases onto someone because of age, financial status, religious or political affiliation, gender, and so on, is the essence of stereotyping—and usually leads to greater misunderstanding and mistrust. Such snap judgments do a disservice to all.

First we must ask the question: Is it really possible to set aside our own biases and agendas? As a wise sage once said, "Pull your own weeds first." One way to break toxic relationship patterns and resolve conflicts is to look within, as well as listen more honestly while cultivating understanding, empathy, trust, and kindness.

For these reasons, we need to be more aware of both how we use our speech and how we listen. This concept, known as wise speech, expands our awareness and helps us use words in a healing and supportive way. The Buddha, for example, believed that speaking needed to meet the following five criteria:

> *It is spoken at the right time. It is spoken in truth. It is spoken affectionately.*
> *It is spoken beneficially. It is spoken with a mind of goodwill.*[10]

Because words are much like a living clay by which we shape our relationships, each person in a relationship needs to take responsibility for his or her own speech. But that's just part of the story, because truly understanding another requires not just wise speech, but needs wise listening and responding. Toward this end, Tool #38, *H.E.A.L. with Cooperative Listening*, is designed to remove the filters of the rigid thinking, dogma, and biases that can distort our view of others.

Mindfulness means stepping out of one's comfort zone and jettisoning old, worn ways of relating. We need not agree with one another, but we can dialogue, which is to reach an understanding "through word." Dialogue is different from discussion, where we often try to persuade others to our point of view. Interestingly, the word *discussion* comes from the same root as the word *percussion*; certainly, banging someone over the head with our way of seeing things—however enlightened or correct we believe our viewpoint to be—doesn't promote long-term harmony or understanding. With dialogue there's the quality of shared mutuality and exploration, surrendering to deeper meaning, and a desire to seek truth together.

It is by engaging in the spirit of shared mutuality and understanding that the tools here can guide relationships toward resolving differences.

---

[10] "Buddhism—Right Speech," http://www.hinduwebsite.com/buddhism/rightspeech.asp (accessed April 2017).

TIPS FOR WORKING WITH CLIENTS

✓ Resolving conflicts is also reflected by how well we can plant the following three important seeds:

- The seed of trust, without which there can be no safety in a relationship.

- The seed of acceptance, which recognizes no one is perfect.

- The seed of empathy, which is a gateway to love and intimacy.

✓ Consider using the following as a conflict resolving package of practices: Tool #23, *Grow Your Compassion Container*, Tool #25, *Using Affirmations as a Relationship GPS*, Tool #36, *Building Trust that Lasts*, Tool #38, *H.E.A.L. with Cooperative Listening*, and Tool #40, *Spontaneous Play*.

✓ Feel free to work with the client to develop a tailored bundle of relationship bonding and enhancing practices that works best for them.

Tip #10	# Embracing a Strengths-Based Approach

THOUGHTS FOR THERAPISTS

Did you ever meet anyone through the "lens" of strengths? In other words, did you get to know someone by focusing in on that person's character strengths? In workshops, I often conduct an exercise where everyone shares a simple story that reveals their strengths. Normally, when clinicians are working with clients they are more tuned in to listening for the problem. Even in the course of your daily interactions, how often do you listen for the strengths in another?

Listening in this way can be uplifting. In fact, it shines an entirely new light on how we employ a host of strengths to accomplish even the smallest things each day. It's easy to think of accomplishments as reaching the large goals in life. But as someone working in the health care field, you can provide a more nurturing and strengths-based way of viewing accomplishments.

Even simple acts of self-care—brushing your teeth, getting enough sleep, and eating nutritious meals—are accomplishments that require the strengths of effort, discipline, and persistence. Even getting dressed in the morning is a highly underrated strength! After all, choosing clothes and dressing each day requires no small degree of forethought, planning, organization, and action. Why not recognize even the small strengths that help us get through the day?

A strengths-based focus has another benefit. It makes us feel productive and enhances positive affect. positive psychology and studies conducted by Martin Seligman have confirmed that the practice of identifying and putting one's "signature strengths" into action daily can have a long-term effect on increasing happiness and reducing depression.[11] Seligman and his associates developed a list of six key virtues, including *Wisdom and Knowledge*, *Courage*, *Humanity*, *Justice*, *Temperance*, and *Transcendence*. Contained within each of these categories are different and unique character strengths, with 24 character strengths in all.

This brings new clarity to how anyone can be empowered through displaying strengths. One useful way to introduce strengths to clients is through Tool #27, *Identifying Strengths to Build Closeness*.

TIPS FOR WORKING WITH CLIENTS

To help clients better understand the concept of strengths, you may want to explore the following ideas:

✓ Focusing on strengths is not a phony ego boost.
  • Character strengths are real, and everyone possesses several.
✓ Exploring how character strengths were viewed in one's family can be a good starting point for exploring how this practice will be received.

---

[11] M. E. P. Seligman, T. A. Steen, N. Park, and C. Peterson, (2005). Positive psychology in progress. Empirical validation of interventions. *American Psychologist*, 2005; 60: 410–421.

✓ Many tools in these pages can be bundled and viewed through the lens of strengths. For example, you might bundle Tool #27, *Identifying Strengths to Build Closeness*, with Tool #24, *S.T.O.P. the Relationship Robot of Reactivity* (strengths of forbearance and regulation), Tool #22, *Get C.U.R.I.O.U.S.* (strengths of curiosity, openness, and non-judging awareness), Tool #21, *The Power of Acceptance and Patience* (strengths of acceptance and patience), and Tool #20, *Self-Soothing and Synchronized Breathing* (the strengths of attunement and equanimity).

✓ Above all, have fun when working with strengths.

Mindfulness Tools for Relationship with Self

Tool #11 | # Optimize Communication with Your Mindful Learning Styles

Mindful Learning Styles

The following learning styles are compatible with this practice:

Verbal-Linguistic   Social-Interpersonal

Visual-Spatial   Reflective-Intrapersonal

Sound-Musical   Natural World

Bodily-Kinesthetic-Tactile   Existential-Meaning

Mathematical-Science-Logical

Note: Each of the tools in *The Mindfulness Toolbox for Relationships* begins with a list of Mindful Learning Styles that fit best with that tool. While this book can be used without using these styles, matching a client's style to a practice can improve its effectiveness. For more information about mindful learning styles, as well as information on how to assess someone's styles, refer to Tip #3, *Identifying and Implementing Mindful Learning Styles.*

THOUGHTS FOR THERAPISTS

As described in Tip #3, *Identifying and Implementing Mindful Learning Styles*, understanding another's style has many benefits. It's like entering the other person's innate language of awareness. From this vantage point you have a deeper understanding of how to communicate and connect with them. And, when you access another's mindfulness language, they will naturally get present and attentive! This knowledge can amplify your ability to relate and work with others. Best of all, it's fairly easy to learn the mindful language of others.

There are two parts to accomplishing this. First is to learn about one's own mindful learning styles. This can be an eye-opening and affirming practice. For example, if someone is visual, that person will know the importance of visually seeing information in order to remember it; simply hearing the information may not be enough for it to sink in.

Secondly, one needs to become more proficient at observing others. The following handout will provide some guidelines for becoming a mindful learning style detective. Being armed with this information can help clients, or anyone, break free from old mindsets and find new ways of relating to important persons in their lives.

TIPS FOR WORKING WITH CLIENTS

Help clients find examples from their own life that illustrate their key mindful learning styles. If there are conflicts with another person, determine if lack of communication is due to a major learning style difference.

✓ One good starting point may be to define mindful learning styles as "the very personal language of how someone gets very present, attentive, and learns most easily."

✓ Explore the advantages of understanding mindful learning styles for communicating and working with others.

✓ Access the following mindful learning style tools mentioned in Tip #3, *Identifying and Implementing Mindful Learning Styles:*

- The book *7 Kinds of Smart: Identifying and Developing Your Multiple Intelligences* by Thomas Armstrong and its assessment.

- *The Joy Compass* by Donald Altman, which matches mindfulness and contemplative practices with the various learning styles.

- Edutopia's *Multiple Intelligences Self-Assessment*
  - https://www.edutopia.org/multiple-intelligences-assessment

- The *Rogers Indicator of Multiple Intelligences*
  - http://www.personal.psu.edu/bxb11/MI/rimi2.htm

Be a Mindful Learning Style Detective

Instructions

Mindful learning styles are much like language. They are a form of communication that is based on the innate ways that someone gets very present and attentive. For example, those who love looking at sunsets, going to art galleries, and watching the latest in fashion tend to be visual. By contrast, those who love dancing, going to concerts, and hearing the ocean waves tend to be sound and music oriented.

There are nine different ways of mindfully getting present—and each of us uses several of these styles. If your partner is accessing one style while you're accessing a different one, it might be hard to communicate or understand the needs of the other person—until you "speak" in their mindful learning style, or at least translate their style in a way that makes sense to you.

This is just an introduction to these styles. To get a more in-depth look at your primary and secondary mindful learning styles, consider looking at these websites:

- Edutopia's *Multiple Intelligences Self-Assessment*
  - https://www.edutopia.org/multiple-intelligences-assessment
- The *Rogers Indicator of Multiple Intelligences*
  - http://www.personal.psu.edu/bxb11/MI/rimi2.htm

Look at this list of the nine different mindful learning styles:

Verbal-Linguistic
Visual-Spatial
Sound-Musical
Bodily-Kinesthetic-Tactile
Mathematical-Science-Logical
Social-Interpersonal
Reflective-Intrapersonal
Natural World
Existential-Meaning

Next, look at the following list and circle the words that describe the types of hobbies, activities, or things you find engaging and enjoyable.

As you do this, think in terms of what you like to do during your free time or what you did on your last vacation. How did you spend your time? This will help you identify how you get present. Remember that mindful learning styles can be mixed. So taking a long walk by yourself on the beach, for example, could be visual-spatial, bodily-kinesthetic, sound-musical, reflective-intrapersonal, and natural world oriented. That's not to say all of these are your primary style of getting present, but an activity might appeal to you because it taps more than one of your getting present styles!

Language/Verbal & Thinking Oriented

Likes the following: analyzing, reflecting, meditating, reading, writing, keeping a journal, crosswords, word games, puns, word jokes, speaking, listening, or telling stories.

Visual/Spatial Oriented

Likes the following: museums, art fairs, looking at sunsets, photography, painting, doodling, quilting, knitting, astronomy, motorcycling, bird watching, watching sports, fashion, looking at the stars, and nature.

Sound/Hearing & Music Oriented

Likes the following: music, concerts, dancing, singing, chanting, playing an instrument, sound of the ocean waves, and sounds of nature.

Bodily/Kinesthetic & Tactile Oriented

Likes the following: dancing, swimming, walking, yoga, stretching, hot baths, jogging, hiking, biking, knitting, weight lifting, painting, sculpting, jewelry making, scrap-booking, competitive and non-competitive sports.

Mathematical/Science & Logical Oriented

Likes the following: Sudoku, numbers, reading, computer programming, analyzing, going to museums, understanding how things work, science, learning, chess, games of strategy.

Social/Interpersonal & Relationship Oriented

Likes the following: friends, committed relationships, volunteering, book clubs, social gatherings, church activities, planning or going to parties, empathizing, teaching, public spaces, team sports.

Reflective/Intrapersonal & Spirituality Oriented

Likes the following: learning about oneself, praying, meditating, reading and reflecting, thinking about purpose and gratitude, going to lectures, spiritual/religious rituals, solitude, seeking out silence, nature, and wisdom.

Natural World Oriented

Likes the following: hiking, hunting, fishing, boating, the beach, camping, sailing, archaeology, natural shapes and objects, sitting in the park, farmers markets, and exploring new locations.

Existential/Meaning Oriented

Likes the following: learning, introspection, expressing ideas rather than rote learning, philosophy, dialogue, reading, prayer, meditation, rituals and ceremonies, transcendent thinking, and deeper meaning.

Reflections

What was it like to identify how you get present? How long have you used this way to get present and express yourself?

_____

_____

_____

Which learning styles do you think are your key ones? When you think about how you best learn, which of these styles helps you to best remember or learn?

_____

_____

_____

Think of someone significant in your life, and underline the activities in the preceding list that you feel fits best with that person. How could an understanding of that person's style help you communicate more effectively with that person? What activities could you enjoy together?

_____

_____

_____

Mindful Learning Style Practice

For the next week, see if you can identify the styles of others. Then, adapt so that you connect by using, or "speaking" their innate style. Notice how this changes the interaction or deepens your understanding of that person. For example, if someone is visual, you might use the phrase "I _see_ what you mean." If someone is verbal-linguistic oriented, you might recall or share stories about an event that occurred. Get creative and notice how your new "language" resonates with your partner or others.

Tool #12	# Body Regulation for Grounding and Attention

THOUGHTS FOR THERAPISTS

As one of the "three regulations" of mindfulness, the body is important for several reasons in terms of relationships. First, accessing the body makes it easier to name and label feelings and emotions. An example of this was a client I worked with, Beth, who would often binge eat at fast food drive-thru restaurants, and she did so to make the uncomfortable feeling in her body go away. When asked to name the feeling, she said she couldn't identify it. For a homework assignment, I asked her to try a simple experiment the next time she felt the urge to binge. Before ordering, she was instructed to wait in the parking lot of the fast food establishment and give a name to the feeling in her body. When Beth returned to the group, she shared the story of how she waited in her car for 40 minutes before she identified the feeling. It was loneliness. This was an epiphany for her, and realizing it wasn't physical hunger, Beth left without ordering and drove back home.

There's also good evidence from the mindfulness research of J. David Creswell that the act of naming an emotion actually inhibits, or quiets down, the amygdala—the part of the brain that triggers the fight and flight stress response.[12] Knowing your emotions gives you a lot more information than just reacting to a feeling.

A second good reason for accessing the body is that it gets someone physically "grounded" in present-moment awareness. This is a good method for getting regulated and centered. Getting into the body can turn one's attention away from the trigger or stress and direct it to the body.

---

[12] J. David Creswell, Baldwin Way, et al., Neural correlates of dispositional mindfulness during affect labeling, *Psychosomatic Medicine*, 2007 Jul–Aug; 69(6): 560–5.

Third, getting into the body can help us learn to be more expressive, and to become more aware of the body's movements and gestures. Body language and facial expressions send messages to those around us all the time, whether we are aware of this or not. There is an old proverb that reflects this deeper understanding:

Couples who love each other tell each other a thousand things without talking.

Finally, the body is often the early signaling system for receiving information. More and more, we're learning how important it is to listen to our "gut instinct." In fact, the enteric nervous system, sometimes called "the second brain," actually develops out of the same clump of fetal tissue as the brain. This gut brain contains 100 million neurons and many of the same neurotransmitters found in the brain. Is it any wonder that stress affects the gut? The following handout can be a positive first step to get out of the mind and drop into the body.

TIPS FOR WORKING WITH CLIENTS

✓ For some clients, getting into the body can be scary. So before doing this or any exercise check on the following. If the client has experienced any of the following conditions, collaborate with the client to start in small steps, just choosing any of the handout exercises that feel safe.

- Has the person experienced physical or sexual trauma?
- Does the client's body movement and posture appear stiff and rigid?
- Is the individual experiencing chronic pain?
- Does the client experience anxiety that is triggered by body sensations?

✓ Be sure to let clients know that the grounding methods here are very gentle and just help bring awareness to the body. At any time, clients are free to stop if they experience distressing feelings that they cannot tolerate.

✓ It can help to demonstrate these and follow along with the client as you guide them through this grounding practice.

✓ Share with clients the above-mentioned benefits of getting into the body before following through with the handout.

✓ Give the handout to the client to take home as a practice guide.

Dropping Into the Body & Naming Emotions

Instructions

Do you tune in to your body throughout the day? Getting familiar with the body is beneficial because the body offers much helpful information. Research shows that dropping into the body can help to quiet the busy mind, get us more aware of our emotions, and even help us grow calmer during times of stress. The practices here are simple, gentle ones that you can use anytime to get more centered or to take a soothing and stress-relieving one-minute body break. As you do this, you may also notice where tension builds up in the body.

The practice consists of two parts. Part 1 is about grounding and getting present in the body. Part 2 is about starting to know emotions through sensing the body. Let's try them now.

Note: This body practice is the first part of an overall Mindfulness Body/Breath/Mind Meditation that uses this tool along with Tool #13, *Breath Regulation for Managing Stress*, and Tool #14, *Mind Regulation for Making Peace with the Mind*. We'll learn these one at a time so you can start slowly, gain more practice, and understand the benefits of each.

PART 1 — *Dropping Into the Body*

Sitting — Have a seat on a comfortable chair. If you want to sit on a cushion or on the ground with your legs crossed, that's perfectly fine.

1. To begin, get grounded, physically connected to the ground, or earth. To do this, press your feet into the floor. You can imagine that you are literally "rooting" yourself to the ground like your favorite tree or plant. Trees are among the largest living organisms on the planet, so imagine yourself strong and planted like a tree.

2. Now you are going to bring awareness to the body. First, take a few moments to notice the position of your knees and legs. Now, move up and notice the position of your hands and arms. They may be at your sides or rested on your legs or lap. Either way, just notice them.

3. Finally, bring awareness to your posture. How are you sitting? Ideally, it is good to have a nice erect but relaxed posture. Imagine, for example, that you were having a cup of tea with the Queen of England. How would you sit with the "Queen Mum"? (Now if that is an anxiety-provoking image for you, just ignore it!)

4. Now you are totally sitting—100 percent devoted to the experience of sitting. If your mind wanders, that's okay. Just gently bring it back to your feet on the floor and the position of your knees, legs, arms, hands, and posture. That's all there is to it.

Natural Sitting and Natural Body. It's perfect just as it is. You don't need to change a thing.

Grounding the Hands — Rub your hands together vigorously for 5–10 seconds or until heat builds up between the palms. As you're doing this, think about the rhetorical question: Is what you're feeling yesterday? Is it today? Of course, there's no denying that what you are experiencing is the present moment. One of the benefits of a physical grounding practice is that it can turn us away from reactivity and negative thoughts to an experience in the body—right here, right now.

Rolling the Shoulders and Head — To release tension, roll your shoulders around (in either direction) at least five times. Do this slowly and when you are finished, let your shoulders come to rest, letting them fall as the tension leaves. Notice their position and how differently they feel after this movement. If you experience any pain, just stop or move your shoulders only as far as you can without discomfort.

Next, lower your head and roll it from side to side, stretching the muscles in your neck. Only go as far as you can comfortably move your head without having any pain.

Overhead Arm Stretch — For the last grounding practice, you are going to slowly move your arms high over your head as you take a nice long in-breath. Imagine your arms rising like the sun in the morning sky. Now, as you exhale, slowly lower your arms, letting them come to rest at your sides. Excellent! Congratulations on practicing body grounding. Again, go only as far as you can without discomfort.

Reflections

What was it like for you to sit in this way? Did you notice that you had fewer thoughts or your mind got quieter when you were really "in" the body?

_____

_____

_____

Did you notice any difference in body tension before and after?

_____

_____

_____

What is one way that a daily mindful grounding practice could help deal with stress?

_____

_____

_____

Grounding is portable and can be done anywhere. How could you create a grounding practice? What would that look like? What challenges or obstacles would you face in implementing this?

_____

_____

_____

PART 2 — *Naming Emotions in the Body*

Instructions

Once you have practiced Part 1 start to tune in to any emotions you may be feeling. If you have never practiced naming or labeling emotions, this may take time for you, so be patient with the process.

For example, anger or frustration might be felt as tightness or clenching in the jaw, the hands, the chest, or another part of the body. Sadness or grief might be experienced as a lump in the throat, heaviness in the gut, or feeling like the weight of the world is on your shoulders. **In particular, use this practice whenever you are upset about something or have had a disruption in a relationship.**

Why is this worth learning? Research shows that if you can *name an emotion, that you can tame the emotion*. This is important in relationships, because it means that you can more easily *respond* rather than just *react*. Naming the emotions lets you think about your feelings, understand yourself better, and express your needs in a more thoughtful way—especially when dealing with difficult emotions and situations.

Sitting — Find a nice, quiet, private place where you can sit. As you sit, start from the bottom of your feet and move upward. Notice where there's any tension or tightness. If you sense something in the body, get curious about that sensation. Is this a familiar feeling? Is it unusual?

If you feel yourself getting tense, just take a nice long breath and exhale slowly. If you can't name the feeling right now, that's okay. You can always try again another time.

Sometimes there may be a feeling in the body that you've experienced for a long time. Gently ease into this sensation, without forcing it. If you feel an emotion arise—even a powerful one—that's okay. Just give that emotion a name. Remember that this is a process, a means of getting more familiar with your body's emotional life, its story, and how it communicates with you.

Reflections

What was it like to name your emotions? What was most challenging?

_____

_____

_____

What is one positive change that could come from knowing your emotions? How could this affect a significant relationship in your life?

_____

_____

_____

Tool #13 | # Breath Regulation for Managing Stress

Mindful Learning Styles

The following learning styles are compatible with this practice:

Bodily-Kinesthetic-Tactile   Sound-Musical

Visual-Spatial   Reflective-Intrapersonal

How important is the breath? Someone once wryly commented that all deaths were caused by the same health problem—the failure of those persons to take one more breath. Humor aside, numerous studies have shown that being present with the breath reduces rumination and mind-wandering. In other words, it strengthens our ability to focus and concentrate. Breathing, because it gets individuals into the body, is a grounding practice that has been shown to decrease fear that is related to body sensations.

In other words, breathing is wonderfully regulating. And, if someone practices diaphragmatic breathing (see Tool #20, *Self-Soothing and Synchronized Breathing*) the stress response gets turned down, which further reduces the presence of stress hormones like cortisol and adrenaline in the body. Belly breathing, or diaphragmatic breathing, helps activate the parasympathetic nervous system. Herbert Benson, who was one of the early mind-body pioneers, termed this "the relaxation response." This response produces the following effects:

- Slows respiration
- Slows pulse rate
- Lowers blood pressure
- Increases alpha brain waves
- Releases serotonin

The purpose of this tool's handout is to get more intimately connected to the breath and to find an "anchor" point in order to maintain focus on the breath. This will not necessarily activate the parasympathetic relaxation response, although that might naturally happen as a by-product of simply relaxing and slowing down.

For diaphragmatic breathing, see Tool #20, *Self-Soothing and Synchronized Breathing*, which explains how to get the breath into the deeper part of the lungs, in addition to describing the physiology behind how this deeper breathing activates the relaxation system using the vagus nerve.

TIPS FOR WORKING WITH CLIENTS

Here are some suggestions for using breathing tools.

✓ To teach the fundamental **Mindfulness Body/Breath/Mind Meditation,** use Tools #12, #13, and #14 in order—and then later bring in Tool #20 as a way of regulating the breath.

✓ If you are just working with breath, consider bundling Tool #13 and Tool #20. Tool #13 will get someone connected to the breath and deal with any anxiety that may occur. Once connected, Tool #20 will teach postures for diaphragmatic breathing—as well as synchronizing the breath with another.

✓ Breathing can be taught to children as easily as to adults.

- If you're working with children, they can connect with breath by blowing on a pinwheel and keeping it spinning for as long as they can—which requires a long, slow breath.

- Children can lie down and can place something light on their belly, such as a stuffed toy or piece of paper. Then, ask them to move the object just by breathing. (Breathing more deeply is easier for anyone—children or adults—when lying down on the back or the side.)

Getting Connected and Curious About the Breath

Instructions

Did you ever think about how many breaths you take in the course of a day? The average person takes between 18,000 to 20,000 breaths a day—and no two of those breaths are alike. Just like snowflakes, each is unique. In this handout, you'll get more curious about the breath.

Sit — To begin, find a seat on a comfortable chair or cushion. You might want to avoid lying down as that could make you drowsy. Basically, you want to get settled into the body before practicing with the breath. So you might want to review the steps in Tool #12 for getting grounded by pressing your feet to the floor; bringing awareness to the positioning of the arms, legs, hands, and feet; and taking a nice erect and dignified but relaxed posture.

Get Curious About the Breath

1. Now you are going to turn your awareness toward the breath. This is an easy practice. Just notice how each breath is slightly different from the one that preceded it. If a breath is longer, just make a note to yourself that "this is a longer breath." If a breath is shorter, note to yourself that "this is a short, or shorter, breath." You can even notice how the pause between each in-breath and out-breath is a little different from the one that came before.

    Now, spend a few moments breathing and noticing the uniqueness of each breath.

2. Now that you've gotten more aware of each breath, it's time to get curious. This means you can notice whatever grabs your attention and go with it! For example, maybe you notice that the in-breath seems to start in a particular part of the body. Or maybe you notice how air feels cool when entering the nasal passages but is warmer when it leaves. There's no right or wrong way to notice the breath because your breath is unique.

    So now, take a few moments to get curious about the breath.

Natural Breathing

1. However you are breathing is perfect just as it is. You don't need to change a thing—isn't that nice to know? Just as the practice of sitting in Tool #12 was about devoting yourself 100 percent to the experience of sitting, you can devote yourself 100 percent to the experience of breathing. This is breathing with a sense of ease, without any effort, and without trying to change anything. And, if your mind wanders off somewhere, that's okay and quite normal. Just gently bring it back to each in-breath and out-breath.

    Remember, this is natural breathing, natural breath, and it's perfect just as it is.

    Enjoy this for a minute or two. Excellent.

Find Your Breath Anchor

1. If someone says to you, "pay attention to the breath," it's easy to get distracted because you don't have anything specific to focus on while breathing. That's why you're going to find an "anchor point" with the breath—a specific place in the body where you most notice or feel the breath. To find this anchor point, you are going to ask yourself the following: *Where in the body do I most vividly notice the physical sensation of breath?*

   There's no one place where people most notice the breath. There are many places, such as at the tip of the nostrils where the air enters, inside the nasal passages, in the back of the throat, in the expansion of the chest or belly, even the movement of the shoulders or the back. Some people experience the breath as a visual color or image. Also, this anchor can be in one place or multiple places.

2. So right now, let's spend a few moments as you find your own personal anchor point with the breath.

   Good. Now that you've found that anchor point, let's see what it's like to stay with it—to focus your attention on it for the full duration of a breath: The in-breath, the pause, and the out-breath. Take that anchor point breath now.

   Placing your attention on this anchor point is an important part of a mindful breathing meditation. But know, too, that your anchor point can change. For example, you might have noticed your breath moving even as you did the anchor practice. It might have started higher in the chest and then dropped into the belly. That's perfectly okay. And it means that you are being present and noticing the anchor point where it is right now. As you continue to practice working with the breath—such as with the belly breathing in Tool #20, *Self-Soothing and Synchronized Breathing*—you might find that the anchor shifts.

Congratulations on exploring your breath! Now that you've learned this skill, you're ready to move on to Part 3 of the Mindfulness Body/Breath/Mind in Tool #14, *Mind Regulation for Making Peace with the Mind.*

Reflections

Where in the body did you most vividly sense the breath? Was this familiar to you? Or was it surprising?

_____

_____

How did having an "anchor point" with the breath help you stay focused?

_____

_____

What did you like most about noticing your breath in this way? What was most challenging?

_____

_____

_____

Tool #14 | # Mind Regulation for Making Peace with the Mind

Mindful Learning Styles

The following learning styles might fit with this practice:

- Bodily-Kinesthetic-Tactile
- Visual-Spatial
- Sound-Musical
- Reflective-Intrapersonal
- Mathematical-Science-Logical
- Existential-Meaning

THOUGHTS FOR THERAPISTS

Much of human suffering comes from how one perceives the world. It's easy to grab onto, or identify with, all kinds of thoughts. We tend to take thoughts more seriously because they come from inside our own heads. But what if there were a way to constructively distance ourselves from thoughts? What if it were possible to not have thoughts pull us in different—and sometimes unhelpful—directions? What if we could just observe them from a safe distance before deciding on their accuracy?

It was over 125 years ago that psychology visionary William James wrote, "The faculty of voluntarily bringing back a wandering attention over and over again, is the very root of judgment, character, and will…An education which should improve this faculty would be the education par excellence. But it is easier to define this ideal than to give practical instructions for bringing it about."[13] James would have been enthralled to know that science now affirms that the mind can be trained in this way. In fact, in a groundbreaking study, researchers measured whether a wandering attention state could affect one of the body's most fundamental units—the telomere. Telomeres are measures of biological aging, and they naturally shorten with age. This study, published in *Clinical Psychological Science*,[14] showed for the first time that a wandering mind—focused on negative thoughts such as rumination or anxiety—could prematurely shorten telomeres. Researchers concluded that focusing on the present moment could actually promote cell longevity. Other research indicates that people report themselves as being happier when they are more present.

The handout here can be used as a stand-alone practice or part of an overall Mindfulness Body/Breath/Mind Meditation using Tools #12, #13, and #14.

TIPS FOR WORKING WITH CLIENTS

✓ Paying attention to the mind can be a surprising experience if one has not done this. It's not uncommon for individuals to be surprised at the number of thoughts they have.

---

[13] William James, *Principles of Psychology* (New York: H. Holt and Company, 1890).
[14] Elissa Epel, Eli Puterman, et al., Wandering minds and aging cells, *Clinical Psychological Science*, 2012, 1(1): 75–83.

✓ Let clients know that the purpose of this practice is not to "empty" the mind of thoughts or to eliminate thoughts. It's okay and normal to have thoughts—and lots of them!

✓ Start small, with this or any practice. Even a one- or-two-minute practice of sitting with thoughts is adequate when beginning. As one practices, it's advisable to increase this to 5 or 10 minutes.

✓ This practice "trains the mind" much like a puppy dog is trained to heel and pay attention.

✓ It is best to let go of expectations when doing this practice. Don't worry about getting it perfect. It's a journey and a process, not an outcome.

Making Peace with the Mind

Instructions

Use this as a stand-alone practice or as part of an overall Mindfulness Body/Breath/Mind Meditation that combines Tools #12, #13, and #14.

The purpose of the Mindfulness Body/Breath/Mind Meditation is to maintain focus on the present moment with whatever is happening in the body, breath, and mind. With the meditation, you'll be focusing attention on the breath, but you'll notice that the mind inevitably wanders off. This may happen a lot, or a little. Either way, when it does, you'll cultivate the ability to simply observe the mind's wanderings, as if from a safe distance. Then, you'll *redirect your attention back to the anchor point with the breath*. It's that easy.

Well, it's not really *that* easy. It takes time, effort, and practice, but wherever you are on this journey, it's the best place for you to be. To begin, do this for two to five minutes, just to see how it feels. Ideally, you can build up to 10 minutes a day to get maximum benefit for helping cultivate constructive distance from thoughts—especially negative ones.

Find a quiet place where you can sit undisturbed. If you have a timer, you can use that to set the length of time.

Sitting — Center in the body as you learned in Tool #12, *Body Regulation for Grounding and Attention*. You can always start by pressing your feet into the floor, noticing the position of your legs, knees, arms, hands, and posture. Allow yourself to feel as if you've come home, fully at rest and grounded in the body.

Breathing — Next, connect with the breath as described in Tool #13, *Breath Regulation for Managing Stress*. Find where you most vividly notice the sensation of breath in the body *right now*. If the anchor point changes, that's okay. What's important is that you have a place to focus attention on as you do this practice.

Getting to Know the Mind — Did you stop to count your thoughts this morning? I like to raise that question in workshops. It usually gets a laugh because the idea of counting our thoughts seems almost impossible. Scientists report a range of thoughts that can be experienced per second— from 25 to 125 thoughts per second. The Buddha thought we could have as many as 3,000 thought moments in a single second. Once, when I mentioned this in a workshop, a participant raised her hand and said, "I have four thousand!" She might be right. As you do this practice have patience, and know that it's okay if you notice a lot of thoughts. Most people do. The idea here is not to stop your thoughts or "empty your mind." Instead, it's just to get to know your thoughts and cultivate awareness of your mind wandering. By noticing when your mind wanders, you'll be able to gently redirect your attention and focus back to the body and the breath.

Disengage from Thoughts by Labeling Mind Wandering — There are many kinds of mind wandering. You might wander off to a thought about the past or something that happened earlier in the day. Maybe you are thinking about something that you have to do later in the day. Or, you might be having a self-referential thought—such as wondering if you're doing this meditation correctly. Even a self-critical thought is just another form of mind wandering that has taken you away from paying attention to the breath.

Fortunately, there's an easy way to disengage from mind wandering and return your focus to the breath. The method is to simply name, or label, your mind wandering. To do this, you can simply think "wandering," "mind wandering," or "thinking." These are very neutral ways of looking at your thoughts. This more objective way of noticing is not blaming or judging. It's just commenting that the thought—whatever kind of thought you have—is a wandering one.

For those who are very visual, you might want to imagine thoughts as clouds floating by in the sky, or as a leaf floating on a stream or river. By letting the cloud or leaf float past, you can disengage and then return to your breath.

Get creative. You might find that just simply "noticing" a thought is enough to let you release it. Or you might use other words or phrases. One person who I worked with and had intrusive anxious thoughts, would simply notice those thoughts and mentally say, "Hello again, old friend." In this way he recognized the thought but didn't react to it, try to fight with it, or heap blame on himself for having an anxious thought. Basically, he changed his relationship to his thoughts! You can, too.

As you do this practice, remember that thoughts are not necessarily facts. They do not define you.

It's also a good practice to **label emotions** as they arise. If you feel an emotion, such as anger, impatience, frustration, or boredom, simply name the emotion. Research shows that naming an emotion is helpful because it lets us process the emotion by examining it with the thinking brain as opposed to just reacting with the emotional part of the brain. Over time, this practice reduces stress related to negative triggers and puts you more in control of how you want to respond to any situation.

Are you ready to start the actual practice? Settle in to your chair or cushion, and start your Mindfulness Body/Breath/Mind Meditation for up to five minutes to start.

Reflections

How busy was your mind during this practice? Remember, it's okay to have thoughts, even lots of them.

_____

_____

_____

What was it like to observe thoughts in a more neutral and impartial way? What method(s) of labeling or disengaging from mind wandering worked best for you?

_____

_____

_____

What was easiest about this practice? What was most challenging?

_____

_____

_____

How could you create a daily Mindfulness Body/Breath/Mind Meditation practice? What would that look like? What challenges or obstacles would you face in implementing this? Remember that you do many things for your physical hygiene each day—brushing your teeth, taking a shower, etc.—so what would it be like to spend a few minutes a day for your mental hygiene?

_____

_____

_____

Note: When starting a Mindfulness Body/Breath/Mind Meditation practice, begin with a structured plan. Include when, where, and for how long you will practice. Consistency is important. So is accountability. So track your practice and let someone know. Another way to stay consistent is to practice with a partner or others. Remember that it's okay to start small and build up. You can always adapt the plan so it works better for you. Even a few minutes a day of this practice can be beneficial in helping find greater emotional peace and calm.

There are also apps that can help you to practice and develop a daily routine, so consider typing "mindfulness" into your app finder and several options will appear.

Tool #15 | # Accepting the Unwanted and Rejected

Mindful Learning Styles

This practice touches upon many learning styles:

Verbal-Linguistic   Mathematical-Science-Logical

Visual-Spatial   Reflective-Intrapersonal

Sound-Musical   Existential-Meaning

Bodily-Kinesthetic-Tactile

THOUGHTS FOR THERAPISTS

Did you ever want to avoid an experience or push something away? Have you ever rejected even a common idea that you found unpleasant or annoying? There are many things that we can try to resist. Here are a few:

- Not getting the recognition you want
- Getting stuck on the freeway
- Hearing a noise when you want quiet
- Not getting fast enough service at a restaurant
- Being sick with a cold or the flu
- Being disappointed by another's actions
- Being disappointed at one's own ability to do/be better
- Your own feelings of uneasiness or anxiety

Of course, this is the short list. There are many more serious life events that are painful at many levels, such as a major illness, a divorce or death of a loved one, the loss of a job or career, and so on. Even for those life-altering negative events, a lot of our suffering comes from trying to resist the conditions with which we are confronted. After all, ask yourself: Doesn't it take a lot of energy and emotion to resist things that cannot be controlled? And here is exactly where acceptance can help. As mentioned in Tip #1, *P.A.I.R. U.P. for Mindful Relationships*, and Tip #2, *Managing Expectations with a Mindful Model of Change*, cultivating an awareness and attitude of acceptance is an essential part of relating to oneself and others with a greater sense of openness, patience, and kindness.

While we may not always choose what life gives us, we *can* choose our attitude and how to respond. Above all, it's important to recognize that acceptance is not giving up, but opening and softening to life. Acceptance is a choice. In essence, it says, "I don't have to beat myself or others over the head when things don't go my way." Acceptance is like the protective Band-Aid or healing salve that you can apply over life's unwanted and unexpected insults, wounds, and other impossible things in order to have time to heal.

TIPS FOR WORKING WITH CLIENTS

Acceptance is a skill that can be practiced and cultivated. Here are a few thoughts to consider for how self-acceptance defuses the egocentric viewpoint and the need to be right.

- ✓ Acceptance does not mean resigning oneself to a situation, but rather, surrendering to the way things are with an open and willing attitude.
  - Submission means resignation; surrender means acceptance.
- ✓ Acceptance helps us gently detach from those areas where we are too constricted and tight.
- ✓ Self-acceptance helps us stop seeing things as black-white and good-bad, but to recognize that all things are mixed. Even our heroes have good and not so good qualities.
- ✓ With acceptance, we can recognize and even appreciate the brokenness and imperfections of others in our life.

Meditation for Resting in Self-Acceptance

Instructions

We're going to use a visualization to find greater acceptance for something in your life—either internal or external—that is causing you pain because you want to resist its presence in your life. You are free to hold onto your pain, of course, but you can also feel free to try this practice and just notice with happens. The idea is to be more willing and accepting of your entire being and the challenging conditions you face.

This practice has two parts. First you'll identify what you don't want to accept right now—that thing that is causing you pain and hurt. Then, in Part 2, you'll use your imagination to see how you might change your perspective on that hurt or challenge.

You can always read through the entire meditation first, or read as you follow along, or record this so that you can easily complete this without referring to the guided script.

PART 1 — *What is one thing that I cannot accept?*

For this practice, think of one thing that you cannot accept. If you want, you can write this on a sheet of paper. What's important is that you identify something specific. It may be related to a physical body problem or worry, an emotion that you have, or a situation you are confronted with. Here are some examples:

- I am getting older, no longer feel attractive, and can't do what I used to do.
- I feel inadequate compared to others.
- I can't find a partner, and I fear being alone.
- I worry about my relationship with a friend, partner, child, co-worker, etc.
- I hate my job/career (fill in the blank) and feel like I'm at a dead-end.
- I was abused and mistreated by _____, and I can't forgive or accept it.
- I have a chronic health issue that I don't deserve and feel defeated by.

PART 2 — *Opening to greater understanding, compassion and self-acceptance*

Follow along with this meditation—eyes closed preferably, as you open to a less harsh perspective, or perhaps a fresh understanding of that thing you can't accept.

Find a quiet place to sit.

Feel Your Benefactors — Slow your breathing. Picture yourself resting in a place of supreme beauty and peace. This can either be a real place that you love—a place in nature—or an imaginary place that you can picture. Nothing here can harm or disturb you, and you feel protected, safe, and calm. If at any time your mind wanders away or has an unpleasant, intrusive thought, that's okay. Simply notice that with acceptance and then release that thought.

Next, think about people who have been benefactors in your life. You know someone is a benefactor because these people want you to be well and happy and safe. And, when you're around such persons you feel good. You may not agree with everything this person says or believes, but you know they wish the best for you! There's no limit to who they might be. They could be friends, family members, kindly neighbors, or even that spiritual person from history who you admire. Picture yourself surrounded by all these well-wishers, knowing that they would be here right now with you if they could.

Let yourself absorb the blessings and kind thoughts these benefactors have for your well-being. In fact, imagine that you are breathing in the wishes for your well-being. You might sense these as a warmth that spreads throughout the body and into your cells. Maybe you feel warmth in the heart center. As you feel these wishes for your safety and well-being, let the glow of caring and love circulate through the body.

Visualize a Bubble of Self-Acceptance — Next, imagine that the warm glow of blessings and love from your benefactors surrounds your being, almost like a protective bubble. See how the bubble's golden glow feels warm, comforting, and inviting. Think of this as your own bubble of self-acceptance. This is a bubble that can safely encompass anything, no matter how difficult or unwanted it may be.

Now, in the far-off distance, see the thing that you noted or wrote down earlier which you cannot accept. In fact, it's so far away that it seems small and insignificant—especially from your vantage point inside the safe bubble of self-acceptance.

Grow the Bubble of Self-Acceptance — Picture the bubble of self-acceptance growing larger and larger, expanding all around you. Even your thoughts, including your emotions—positive or negative—are now surrounded by the bubble, letting you just sit in an accepting and safe way with them all. Feel a sense of expansion, spaciousness, and peace as the bubble continues to grow.

As the bubble of self-acceptance grows, it naturally takes more and more inside of it. Once anything is inside the bubble you no longer have to react to it, but can freely notice it with kindness, greater understanding, and compassion.

The bubble is infinite in how far it can grow, and you are in control of the bubble as you let it expand farther and farther, until it finally gets all the way out to that difficult thing that you cannot accept. Let the bubble touch and make contact with the unwanted thing. Notice what this feels like. Then, let the bubble soften as it makes contact so that it can allow that difficult thing inside. The bubble naturally wants to bring everything inside because it is accepting in the same way that a loving parent, best friend, compassionate mentor, or spiritual teacher accepts you for who you are. There's nothing that the bubble can't accept.

Rest with the All-Inclusive Bubble of Self-Acceptance — As you come to peace and at rest with all that is inside the bubble—even that difficult thing—see the bubble growing even more. Watch as it expands far beyond the horizon of the beautiful place where you sit. Now, everything is within the bubble. There is no more inside or outside, no more pushing or pulling, no more good or bad you, no more winning or losing, in this all-inclusive, self-accepting and loving place.

Continue to breathe slowly for as long as you like. Know that your benefactors are still safely beside you, guiding you.

Set a Wise Intention — You now have it within your power to set an intention to accept and view your difficult situation not as an end point, but as a **starting point.** A point from which to grow and learn. Allow your own wisdom to take root and guide you with regards to moving forward.

Now it is time to bid farewell to your bubble of self-acceptance. To do this, send appreciation to your bubble and the kind benefactors and mentors who facilitated this experience and helped you feel safe. Know that you can return to this bubble and experience its warmth, safety, and self-acceptance anytime you need help with facing those unwanted and rejected things.

Reflections

What was it like to feel yourself in a bubble of self-acceptance?

_____

_____

_____

How did this change your perspective of the unwanted thing in your life?

_____

_____

_____

What was hardest about this guided visualization practice? What was easiest?

_____

_____

_____

How and when could you use this practice in the future? What is one way this could help in a relationship in your life?

_____

_____

_____

Tool #16 | Open the Compassionate Heart

Mindful Learning Styles

The following learning styles are compatible with this practice:

Visual-Spatial   Reflective-Intrapersonal

Sound-Musical   Natural World

Bodily-Kinesthetic-Tactile

THOUGHTS FOR THERAPISTS

With the problems and conflicts in the world, Jackie DeShannon got it right in her 1965 hit song, "What the World Needs Now Is Love." That song, with lyrics by Hal David and music composed by Burt Bacharach, was even played as an audio vigil on Los Angeles radio stations after the assassination of Robert Kennedy in 1968.

Interestingly, an analysis of two eras, 1968–1971 and 2002–2005, found that love songs predominated the Billboard top 10 lists during those periods.[15] During the classic rock era, 50 percent of songs were love-related, while that number rose to 60 percent for the more recent time period—though the language of love got a little more risqué and raunchy!

Still, must we wait for tragedy to point out the need for love and compassion? Fortunately, research has shown that compassion can be learned as a skill that actually changes the brain and engages the same circuitry involved in empathy.[16] In the practice that follows, developing compassion is in the form of a Loving-Kindness Meditation. The words used in this meditation have been shown to prime individuals for feelings of safety and trust. This is important not just for transforming relationships with those in our immediate world, but for transforming the relationship we have with ourselves, and with the world at large.

Focusing on loving-kindness and compassion in this way is a bridge to other forms of love. In *How to Love*, Thich Nhat Hanh wrote, "True love is made of four elements, loving-kindness, compassion, joy, and equanimity…If your love contains these elements, it will be healing and transforming, and it will have the element of holiness in it."[17] In Buddhist practice, these four qualities are known as "The Divine Abodes," the mental states that are expressed by enlightened ones. Fortunately, because our neurons wire up by what is in the field of focused attention, we don't need to wait for that enlightened moment to come. All we need to do is practice and let our neurons do the rest!

---

[15] Love still dominates pop song lyrics, but with raunchier language, http://news.ufl.edu/archive/2007/05/love-still-dominates-pop-song-lyrics-but-with-raunchier-language.html (accessed April 2017).

[16] Antoine Lutz, Julie Brefczynski-Lewis, et al., Regulation of the neural circuitry emotion by compassion meditation: Effects of meditative expertise, *Public Library of Science One*, 2008, 3(3): e1897.

[17] Thich Nhat Hanh, *How to Love* (Berkeley, CA: Parrallax Press, 2014), p. 16.

A compassion practice points out the truth that we are more alike than dissimilar. All persons suffer hardships. And so we can soften to others by opening our hearts and realizing that everyone wants to feel safe, secure, and be happy. For that reason, the Loving-Kindness Meditation that follows is a wholesome practice that can overcome our modern world's cynicism and mistrust.

TIPS FOR WORKING WITH CLIENTS

This practice can be adapted and used anytime throughout the day. Also, for those who may not like the word "meditation," this can be thought of as an affirmation practice in which you are training the brain to align with positive thoughts.

✓ For those who have an insecure attachment style, find out what types of words help them feel safe.

- For example, if words like *closeness, acceptance*, and *caring* help someone feel more secure, add those words into the Loving-Kindness Meditation.

✓ Consider teaching this practice along with Tool #19, *Resilience and Sharing a Story of Hope*, Tool #20, *Self-Soothing and Synchronized Breathing*, Tool #21, *The Power of Acceptance and Patience*, and Tool #23, *Grow Your Compassion Container*.

✓ Couples, partners, or others can do this practice together, even holding hands or facing one another as they mentally state the affirming words.

Loving-Kindness and Compassion Meditation

Instructions

In this practice, you will learn some affirming thoughts for the well-being of yourself and others. But let's start by clarifying what the term loving-kindness really means. The kind of love referred to here is not the love bestowed upon specific persons, times, or situations, such as is the case with romantic, sentimental, and nostalgic love. Instead, loving-kindness is non-discriminatory and meant for all persons. It is your unconditional wish for all beings to experience health, safety, and goodwill. And, since loving-kindness naturally includes the idea of forgiveness, this practice will begin with a forgiveness statement. If you feel you are not ready to forgive yourself and always hold back on this, you may want give it a try and see how this feels. Also, it might help to explore Tool #35, *The Gift of Forgiveness*.

Finally, feel free to adapt the words to fit you better. Not only will this practice focus and stabilize your concentration, it will align you with an appreciation for the tenderness and preciousness of life.

Loving-Kindness and Compassion Meditation (Affirmation)

Forgiveness

Find a quiet place where you will not be interrupted. Sit in nature or looking out upon nature if possible. Start with forgiveness, saying the following words:

> May I forgive myself for hurting others, either intentionally or unintentionally.
>
> May others forgive me for hurting them, either intentionally or unintentionally.
>
> May I forgive myself for hurting myself, either intentionally or unintentionally.

Loving-Kindness Toward Oneself

Do this entire practice for about five minutes to start. Of course, if you want to do it longer than five minutes, go for it!

Repeat the following words until you feel a sense of lightness or well-being in the body. As you say these words, you can imagine or picture those who care about you—and who would express these same wishes for you. These persons may be family members, friends, even spiritual people you admire who would send you these wishes for your safety if they could be with you now.

> May I be well.
>
> May I be happy.
>
> May I be safe.
>
> May I be healthy.
>
> May I be peaceful.

Loving-Kindness Toward Family/Friends/Mentors

Now you will send out these wishes to those who have been benefactors in your life. These are persons who, when you are near them, make you feel safe and secure. You could even substitute the words "my family" or "my friends" instead of naming individuals. As you send out this blessing for the well-being of others, picture these persons looking happy and radiant.

May _____ be well.

May _____ be happy.

May _____ be safe.

May _____ be healthy.

May _____ be peaceful.

Loving-Kindness Toward Additional Groups

Next you will send out blessings to the following groups:

- Neutral Persons — these are people whom you may see in your daily life but have no strong connection to.
- Unfriendly Persons — these are individuals who may be family members or associates, but who you don't feel close to. And yet, even they would benefit from this blessing for their well-being.
- All Persons — you can extend your compassion blessing to all persons, and even imagine this blessing spreading outward, from your neighborhood to your county, to your state, to all states, to the continent, and to the entire world.

Closing Statement

It can be helpful to conclude this practice with the following, which is part the ancient, traditional loving-kindness practice.

May suffering ones be suffering free.

May the fear struck fearless be.

May grieving ones shed all grief.

May all beings find relief.

Reflections

What was it like to spend five minutes in this way? How did these words make you feel?

_____

_____

_____

If you could add in other words to the affirmation such as *may I be accepted, may I be understood,* or *may I be loved,* what might they be? Feel free to write down a new version of this practice using these new words.

_____

_____

_____

How could this practice help you to feel more open to life and others?

_____

_____

_____

You don't have to be in a seated meditation to use this practice. Where and when could you mentally say these words to help you get centered and more open?

_____

_____

_____

What is one way that this Loving-Kindness and Compassion Meditation practice could positively change a relationship in your life?

_____

_____

_____

Tool #17 | # Sensing and Honoring the Body

Mindful Learning Styles

The following learning styles are compatible with this practice:

Visual-Spatial   Reflective-Intrapersonal

Sound-Musical   Natural World

Bodily-Kinesthetic-Tactile

THOUGHTS FOR THERAPISTS

It's been estimated that as many as 45 million persons go on a diet every year. Over $33 billion is spent on weight loss. The preoccupation with dieting, coupled with an increasing obesity rate, tells us that a lot of persons are dissatisfied with their body image, especially the size and shape of their bodies. The good news is that they are motivated to do something about it. But when we get overly focused on the outer, superficial form of the body, we can overlook the other benefits that the body provides.

For example, what about appreciating how well the body works each day so that our dreams and goals can be achieved? What about honoring the information offered through the body's felt sense of emotional tone and well-being? What about optimizing the body's unique ability to express feelings to others through movement, gestures, and touch?

The body represents an entirely other language; the more aware we are of body movement, attitude, touch, and inner felt sense, the greater our resilience. This is not a new idea, and over a hundred years ago, Jung promoted the idea of dance, movement, and artistic creativity for getting in touch with our emotions. One study—using healing dance and movement to work with women who had suffered various kinds of abuse—found three key themes emerged as these women learn to cope: "empowerment, healing, and a connection to Spirit."[18]

TIPS FOR WORKING WITH CLIENTS

The following handout integrates different forms of mindful sense-grounding and utilizes all the five senses.

✓ As a prelude to this practice, you may want to start with Tool #12, *Body Regulation for Grounding and Attention*. This will familiarize the client with the basic process of getting grounded in the body.

---

[18] Johanna Leseho and Lisa Rene Maxwell, Coming alive: Creative movement as a personal coping strategy on the path to healing and growth, *British Journal of Guidance & Counselling*, February 2010; 38(1): 17–30.

✓ If desired, Tools #12 and Tool #17 could be bundled together, along with Tool #20, *Self-Soothing and Synchronized Breathing*.

✓ Grounding is often a good means of turning away from negativity and trauma. However, it's important to let clients know that if any unpleasant memories are triggered during physical grounding, they can stop at any time. They can always return to try the practice another time.

Sensing and Honoring the Body Practice

Instructions

By sensing and honoring the body in this way, you can tune in to the vast array of subtle inner feelings, sensations, and emotions that this marvelous container holds.

Find a quiet place where you won't be interrupted. Feel free to do this out in nature. Ideally, do this practice while standing because it will give you more opportunity to move about. But it will work with sitting as well.

If it is helpful, put on some soothing music that your body can move to in a flowing way. In addition, consider using a scented candle, essential oils, or aromatherapy products that help your body relax. **Take as long as necessary to go through these steps. But this can also be accomplished in just a minute or two.**

Breathe through the Whole Body

Take a nice, soothing breath to calm the body and mind. As you inhale, raise your arms up over your head like the sun rising in the morning sky. Wiggle your fingers as they point up to the sky and hold the breath for just a few seconds. Then EXHALE SLOOOWLY as you gently lower your arms.

Take two more of these soothing breaths. With each inhalation, picture the air coming in and filling up the entire body—from the soles of your feet all the way up through the body and to the top of the head. With each exhalation, picture the breath carrying away any tightness or impurities down the body, out of the bottom of the feet, and back into the earth for recycling.

Sensational Sensing

Right now, imagine you possess the senses of a superhero. Use all your senses to expand awareness of your surroundings. For example, it was found that people were able to follow the scent of chocolate on a grassy field using their noses. Humans can sense up to a trillion scents, and track scents just like dogs. What smells do you notice? What's the temperature of the air?

Move about your space as you expand your awareness 360 degrees. Notice as many little details of things as you can. Even if you know the space you're in, surprise yourself. You may even notice microenvironments as you move about. Let your feet feel every little crack or tilt of the ground. Listen for every little sound, hum, and squeak. Let yourself be amazed at the instrument of sensibility you possess!

Tap the Body's Wisdom

Now, let's listen in to your body's needs. As you listen inwardly, notice if there's a wise voice of self-care or self-compassion telling you how to care for the body and take care of yourself. You can scan the body, starting from the bottom of the feet and moving up the body slowly, taking care to open up to any message that is there for you.

Where in the body is there tightness? Where in the body is there heaviness? Where is the body armored or guarded? If you notice something, allow yourself to sense it more deeply. If it had a color, what color would it be? How light or heavy? How long has this feeling been in the body?

As you listen in, let your body know that you are a friend who is coming to visit. There is nothing for either of you to be afraid of. If there is emotion, let yourself sit with it. Let it become softer and less hard, as you continue to just sit with it—being compassionate for how the body has stored emotions for you. But you can also help it to release emotion(s) when it and you are ready.

Move and Observe with Grace

Spend a few moments now moving freely about the space. Now, imagine for a moment that you could watch your body from above, such as from atop a high hill. From this vantage point, observe how the body moves about with grace and dignity. In fact, imagine you can witness all that the body does for you on a daily basis. Watch how it moves around and follows your commands so that you can accomplish your goals each day. Notice how it connects with others. What movements and gestures does it make when with others? Is it welcoming? Standoffish?

Also, notice the signals your body sends you, such as its need for food or touch. How do you respond to these signals? What triggers does your body react negatively to? A lot of what we think is due to feelings may actually originate in the body.

Finally, observe how you take care of the body. How do you encourage it to sleep? How do you help it eat nutritiously? How do you guide it to connect with others?

Honor and Smile Inwardly

Lastly, allow yourself to deeply honor and connect with the sacred inner self. This is how the body gives you a sense of well-being. Breathe into the body, your home. Move about or just be in silence with the sacredness of the body. When you openly listen to the body in this way, you let the body's wisdom communicate to you.

If you want, imagine smiling inwardly at the body, your intimate life partner, as you bathe it in the warm glow of appreciation and gratitude. Let this warm glow of thankfulness seep into all the cells of the body. Rest with this as long as necessary.

Reflections

What was it like to spend a few minutes with the body in this way?

_____

_____

_____

Which of the honoring the body meditation elements was most helpful? What was one new thing that you learned or experienced?

_____

_____

_____

How could this practice help you to connect more with your body, care for your body, or create a close emotional connection with others?

_____

_____

_____

When and how would be good for you to bring this meditation into your day?

_____

_____

_____

Note: You don't have to spend a long time tapping into the body. A speed practice can be done in as quickly as a minute or two. The more frequently that you check in with your gut intuition, or the felt sense of the body, the more you will hear the body's wisdom communicating with you about what is right, good, or safe for you.

Tool #18 | # Stand Up and Know Your Needs

Mindful Learning Styles

The following learning styles are compatible with this practice:

- Verbal-Linguistic
- Visual-Spatial
- Sound-Musical

- Bodily-Kinesthetic-Tactile
- Social-Interpersonal
- Existential-Meaning

THOUGHTS FOR THERAPISTS

Everyone has experienced the playground bully in one form or another. The bully knows how to intimidate, get in someone's space (and face), and act aggressively. The bully doesn't have to be a large person, either. Even the smallest person in a family or relationship can use anger or the threat of anger to control others. So, you can tiptoe around or appease the bully in order to avoid an unpleasant confrontation, but that only emboldens the bully and causes the abuse to continue.

The story of how modern day pilgrim Ann Sieben has dealt with bullies says a lot about standing your ground for what you believe in. In an interview, Sieben described how her many treks carried her to over forty countries and covered thousands of miles.[19] Occasionally, she ran into bullies, or more aptly, men with guns. She recounted the time, in a desolate area of the Mexican desert, where she was confronted by eight drug traffickers who were driving a pickup with several guns mounted on it. Seeing her, they jumped out, and surrounded her with their guns all pointed at her head.

How would you respond to such a dire situation? What Ann did was laugh—at the absurdity of surrounding an unarmed woman with such an overpowering display of force. Now, I'm not saying that laughter is the answer to halt a bully in his or her tracks. But Ann makes the point that her laughter was authentic. It was as if she were saying, "Are you kidding me? You think I'm so dangerous you need to pull eight weapons on me?"

The key point here is that Ann did not let herself be overcome with fear or act aggressively. Instead, she stood calm and steadfast in her truth: She shared that she was simply a pilgrim, and that there was nothing they could really do to harm her. She would either pilgrimage to the site in Mexico where she was headed, or these men would send her on a pilgrimage to heaven. From a mindfulness perspective, she kept her amygdala, the part of the brain that triggers fight and flight, in check. This allowed her to access her thinking brain. Believe it or not, her authenticity and clarity in the moment touched these gun-toting bullies. They actually ended up asking this pilgrim to pray for them.

---

[19] Guri Mehta, A conversation with Ann Sieben, the winter pilgrim, *Parabola*, July 2017: 45–51.

We can learn a lot from people who stand up to bullies without resorting to the tactics of the bully. This takes courage, naturally, as well as a plan and the right resources. However, if a bully has a history and potential for violence, individuals will need to seek professional help and protection.

The following handout asks more questions than it answers, and it is a starting point for someone wanting to stand up and have a voice. It also brings in the idea of cognitive embodiment as discussed in Tip #6, *Working with the Body and Interpersonal Attunement.*

TIPS FOR WORKING WITH CLIENTS

✓ Standing up for one's needs is about setting boundaries and being respected by others.

✓ Boundaries in relationships are important because they are based on a person's needs in a relationship.

✓ It can help to explore someone's family history around establishing healthy boundaries. What did boundaries look like? Were they fair? Consistent?

✓ Consider packaging this tool with some of the breathing practices like Tool #13, *Breath Regulation for Managing Stress*, and Tool #25, *Using Affirmations as a Relationship GPS*. Using a positive affirmation and calming the breath are good ways of clarifying needs and boundaries while staying focused and emotionally steady. In addition, learning Tool #16, *Open the Compassionate Heart*, can help soften one's perspective on others as they stand up.

Compassionately Standing Up

Instructions

When you think about it, boundaries define almost everything in life. Most laws are about boundaries—letting people know what they can and can't do as a way of keeping the peace. But in our private lives there are no clear laws for setting personal boundaries. When others don't respect your boundaries—or you don't respect and heed theirs—that's when conflict occurs and relationships can fray.

Boundaries work best when they are clear and consistent. If others don't have a clear roadmap of your boundaries, or if your boundaries change day to day, there will be misunderstandings.

Everyone has the right to have his or her needs and boundaries respected. Bullying or disrespect can happen no matter how old you are, and no matter *who* you are. Even the Buddha was verbally mistreated, but stood his ground and refused to accept the abuse. Being a kind and compassionate person does not mean you can't stand up for yourself. In fact, that's exactly when it's important to stand up. The following reflections might shed some light on how to firmly stand up, yet still be understanding.

Reflections

What does it physically look like when you stand up for yourself? What is your posture? What movements or gestures do you use? Is your posture defensive or aggressive? Or is it assured, strong, and assertive?

_____

_____

_____

Which of these postures would you *prefer* to use? Which ways of holding the body would best express the way you want to come across as you make your points?

_____

_____

_____

What emotions do you feel when you stand up for yourself? Fear? Worry? Anger? Impatience? Frustration? Doubt? What would it feel like if you could feel a sense of calm, confidence, and clarity in those moments of standing up?

_____

_____

_____

When you stand up, what does your face feel like and what does your voice sound like? Are your face and jaw tight or loose? Is your voice loud or soft, angry or composed, pressured or calm?

_____

_____

_____

What exactly are you standing up for? Why does this situation you are standing up for matter to you? What needs are you addressing (self-care, respect, honesty, etc.)?

_____

_____

_____

Follow-Up Action

Mental rehearsal using visualization is a very effective means for learning new behaviors. Spend five minutes a day for the next week picturing yourself standing up the way you would like. It can help to integrate diaphragmatic breathing, found in Tool #20, *Self-Soothing and Synchronized Breathing*, into the visualization.

Picture yourself stating your needs as your body posture remains confident and assertive. Feel your face and hear your relaxed and expressive voice saying what needs to be said and clearly expressing why this matters to you (and the other person). Know too, that whatever happens, you don't have to react, but can choose to respond calmly.

Additionally, by practicing Tool #16, *Open the Compassionate Heart*, you can recognize and be understanding of the suffering of another—while at the same time compassionately standing up for your own well-being and needs.

Congratulations for exploring standing up for yourself—an important step that requires patience, persistence, and practice.

Tool #19 | # Resilience and Sharing a Story of Hope

Mindful Learning Styles

The following learning styles are compatible with this practice:

Verbal-Linguistic

Reflective-Intrapersonal

Existential-Meaning

Social-Interpersonal

Mathematical-Science-Logical

THOUGHTS FOR THERAPISTS

Anyone in a relationship knows that there will be high points and low points. Some relationships safely navigate the inevitable stormy weather while others are unable to recover. Relationships can be challenging, which is why resilience, optimism, and hope are necessary for any relationship to thrive and grow in the long term.

Resilience is the ability to recover from and bounce back from loss, disappointment, betrayal, and failure. The writings and research of Martin Seligman have focused on how hope serves as an avenue for nurturing feelings of resilience, optimism, and even happiness.[20] Resilience plays an important role because bouncing back from a challenge gives us optimism and hope for the future. It offers evidence that recovery is possible, even under the most difficult of situations.

There may be no sure-fire approach to maintaining relationship resilience, but fostering hope through a story of resilience can cultivate the ability to tolerate the ebb and flow of relationships.

TIPS FOR WORKING WITH CLIENTS

✓ What history of resilience do clients have? How have they recovered from past problems and roadblocks?

✓ Acceptance and patience are a lot about building up the ability to sit with things without having to instantly "fix" them.

✓ Consider bundling this practice with Tool #15, *Accepting the Unwanted and Rejected*, along with Tool #16, *Open the Compassionate Heart*, and Tool #21, *The Power of Acceptance and Patience*.

---

[20] Martin Seligman, *Learned Optimism* (New York: Knopf, 1991).

A Story of Hope and Resilience

Instructions

Here is an opportunity for you to tap into your history for a story that illustrates your own resilience in the face of defeat and failure. Resilience is about how you are able to recover and bounce back from loss or roadblocks that keep you from reaching your goals. In terms of a relationship, resilience means that you can tolerate disappointment, loss, or other ups and downs. Every relationship will ebb and flow, and resilience means that you have the strength to keep trying. It lets you maintain a sense of hope and optimism for the future.

Write your own story of resilience below. After, you can share that with another person, or partner, and have them share their story of resilience with you. When you share a story of resilience, you are also sharing hope and optimism.

Describe a Challenge You Overcame

Right now, think of a time in your life when you were faced with obstacles that blocked you from reaching a goal—but **which you were able to overcome with the help of others.** Maybe you haven't thought about this kind of a story before, but if you look long and hard, you will find that you have overcome many challenges in your life. For example, did someone ever help you in the workplace, or in some other area of your life? Provide a basic, objective, step-by-step description of what happened:

_____

_____

_____

_____

_____

_____

Now, let's examine this story from an emotional point of view. At your lowest point, when it seemed like you couldn't get through this situation or reach your goal—what emotions did you go through? However distressing these were, write them down here:

_____

_____

_____

Next, let's look at the positive emotions. What did you feel like when you got the help and/or resources you needed to overcome the roadblocks in your way? Did you feel happy, optimistic, and hopeful? Write down those happy emotions here:

_____

_____

_____

Reflect on a relationship situation that is distressing or difficult for you right now. How could your story of resilience give you hope or optimism?

_____

_____

_____

Follow-Up Action

As an optional practice, share your story of resilience, using the previous steps, with another. Then, have that person go through the identical steps for sharing a story of resilience and hope with you. In addition, start noticing other stories from your life where you have been resilient and found others to support your goals and efforts.

Reflections

How does sharing and hearing a story of hope with an important person in your life make you both feel? What is it like to know that you have a history of finding resources and having resilience? Together, discuss how this knowledge can be helpful for your relationship.

_____

_____

_____

Tool #20 | Self-Soothing and Synchronized Breathing

Mindful Learning Styles

The following learning styles are compatible with this practice:

Verbal-Linguistic   Reflective-Intrapersonal

Bodily-Kinesthetic-Tactile   Social-Interpersonal

Sound-Musical

THOUGHTS FOR THERAPISTS

Breathing diaphragmatically is critical for relationships because during periods of arguments and feeling defensive, listening becomes harder, if not impossible. That's the biological result of input from the ear traveling from the auditory nerve and right to the amygdala—the brain's emotional safety detector that triggers the fight-flight response. The amygdala's job is to protect us against possible threats—like a tiger growling in the jungle. But that automatic stress response doesn't help us when we're hearing criticism or having a dispute with another person.

Fortunately, breathing quiets down the amygdala and helps us listen again. It's so effective in doing so that the Navy SEALS teach it to new recruits as a means of arousal control and keeping the thinking brain online.

Diaphragmatic breathing, also known as belly breathing, is appreciated and understood in all cultures as a way to cope with stress. Once, when teaching a multicultural group of Mercy Corps leaders, I asked if breathing was accepted in the many cultures represented in the group. One man, from Pakistan, responded that in a country beset by many tragedies, it was a common practice for someone to help others by saying, "take a breath, take a breath."

As children, we naturally breathe into the lower part of the lungs. But encountering stress causes that breath to go into the chest—a more shallow breath that is associated with the sympathetic nervous system and the release of stress hormones into the body and the brain. The good news is that there are some easy postures that make it easy for anyone to return to belly breathing.

TIPS FOR WORKING WITH CLIENTS

✓ It can be helpful to explain the physiology behind diaphragmatic breathing and the relaxation system in the body. See Tool #13, *Breath Regulation for Managing Stress*, for details on how this system works, and the various ways that it slows everything down.

✓ Even if someone says they know how to breathe diaphragmatically, do a visual check to make sure that when they breathe, the belly, and not the chest, is moving predominantly. It's important to see if they learned this properly.

✓ Demonstrate the postures with the client, and see which ones work best. Most people find that one or two of these postures work best for them.

✓ As a final step, problem-solve with clients how they can bring this practice into their day, and into their relationship. It can be a good practice to use this breathing when talking about subjects that could be triggering.

Diaphragmatic
Breathing and Synchronized Breathing

Instructions

Have you seen babies breathe? The belly moves out when they inhale, not the chest. Belly breathing, or diaphragmatic breathing, is how we all naturally breathe. This type of breathing relaxes us and helps us listen better—which is especially important when you're having a disagreement or argument with someone.

Below are five postures that will help you more easily breathe into the belly. This automatically turns on the body's relaxation system, which slows everything down. You'll feel more at ease, open, and less defensive when you breathe like this. As always don't force the breath. Just breathe naturally.

Follow along with each posture. As you do, notice which helps you more easily take that longer, fuller breath. There are two parts to this handout. In Part 2, you can try to synchronize your belly breathing with another person.

PART 1 — *Diaphragmatic Breathing*

Posture 1 — *Hands Behind the Back*

Standing or sitting, place your arms behind your back and clasp your hands together. When you do this, you stretch muscles that run through the rib cage—the intercostal muscles. All these postures stretch the intercostal muscles. This hinges the ribs open and makes it easier to take a deeper, fuller breath.

Notice if there's movement in the abdominal area. If you learned to 'suck it in,' give yourself permission to relax the abdominal muscles. You might even say the word "soft" as you breathe in—just letting the belly muscles relax and release a little bit.

Posture 2 — *Hands at the Sides*

Finding the lowest rib, position both hands at that lowest rib with your elbows facing out. As you breathe, you will notice the sides of the abdomen moving outward. Belly breathing expands the abdominal cavity in all directions. This posture can be good for anyone who doesn't want to focus on the belly moving outward.

Posture 3 — *Hands Behind the Neck/Head*

Clasp your hands behind your head or neck. If that's too difficult, you can alternately just raise your arms and touch your shoulders with your fingertips.

Posture 4 — *Bellows Breathing*

For this posture, place your palms together, chest high. Now you are going to use your arms like a bellows that opens as you inhale and closes as you exhale. As you open the bellows by moving the arms to your sides, take a nice, full belly breath. Keep your arms at your sides as you hold your breath for the count of two or three. Next, exhale slowly on the count of four as you bring the arms together and close the bellows.

Posture 5 — *Butterfly Breathing*

With your hands clasped under your chin, you will use your arms like butterfly wings, flapping them up as you inhale and down as you exhale. Take a long, slow breath as you raise your elbows (butterfly wings). Hold for the count of two or three. Then exhale slowly as you gently lower your butterfly wings.

PART 2 — *Synchronized Breathing*

Synchronized breathing is a nice way for two persons to experience a state of calm together. This can be helpful anytime you and a partner have experienced stress—alone or together—as a way to regulate and attune with one another.

It will help if partners learn the diaphragmatic breathing using the different methods above. Also, remove any heavy clothing, like sweaters or jackets. Then follow these steps:

Step 1 — *Sit Back to Back and Feel Supported*

This works best sitting on cushions or on the floor where the partners' backs can touch. To begin, let yourself gently come into contact with your partner. Gently move back and forth and even side to side, without pushing too hard. This is not a pushing match, but a kind and gentle way of feeling how you are supported and in sync with your partner. Let yourself respond to the movements of your partner until you almost feel as if you are one, very much in touch and in tune.

Step 2 — *Sense and Synchronize the Breath*

Come to rest, with your backs gently touching, bring awareness to your breath and breathe diaphragmatically. As you do so, notice the subtle breathing of your partner. Notice how their breath goes in and out. Let yourself melt into that breath until you are matching your partner's breathing. Don't think too hard about this. If you have thoughts, see if you can just release them and let them go. Come back to your breath and synchronizing your breath with that of your partner. Allow yourself to flow in this way, moving breath-to-breath, effortlessly. Do this for up to five minutes.

Step 3 — *Sit and Face One Another*

Without speaking—turn toward each other. Continue to match your breathing while not touching. Allow your gaze to grow soft as you look at one another. Continue in this way for another three to five minutes. If you would like to touch hands during this phase, that is acceptable, but do so without words, and continue to breathe in a synchronized way.

Step 4 — *Honor and Thank Your Breathing Partner*

To conclude this exercise, place your hands at your heart center and say a mental thanks to your partner for being present with you during this practice.

Reflections

What was it like to move and flow with another person in this way? What did you notice most? What was hardest or easiest about this?

_____

_____

_____

How did it feel to synchronize your breath with another? What feelings did you have when you felt yourself in sync with another?

_____

_____

_____

How could this practice be useful in the future? When could you use it with others?

_____

_____

_____

Mindfulness Tools
for Relationships with
Friends, Family & Lovers

Tool #21 | # The Power of Acceptance and Patience

Mindful Learning Styles

Acceptance and patience are concepts and practices that span the entire range of learning styles:

Verbal-Linguistic   Social-Interpersonal

Visual-Spatial   Reflective-Intrapersonal

Sound-Musical   Natural World

Bodily-Kinesthetic-Tactile   Existential-Meaning

Mathematical-Science-Logical

THOUGHTS FOR THERAPISTS

The qualities of acceptance and patience are recurring themes in *The Mindfulness Toolbox for Relationships*. After all, who hasn't done something worthy of annoyance and irritation? Who hasn't pushed another's buttons, either intentionally or unintentionally? Given that we'd like others to have patience and acceptance for our human quirks and frailties, why not extend these kind offerings to others? And yet these qualities are not easy to master. There's no quick fix or light switch that can turn these on when we need them. They are the result of a long process of a mature exploration, understanding, and practice.

Acceptance and patience are inseparable twins because together they help us deal with what we cannot change. In that way they give us some control over those impossible obstacles that life sometimes places in our path. Neither of these twins are passive.

Acceptance and patience provide an active means of moving through a challenge and giving yourself the time necessary to reach a new perspective.

Acceptance and patience are empowering, too, because they liberate us from feeling we have to act *right now*. Sometimes it's more prudent to wait, to think things out, or see how things develop. Further, acceptance and patience can loosen the hold of rigid expectations that bind us in place. It would be a mistake to interpret these qualities, however, as a reason for allowing abuse or mistreatment.

Another aspect of acceptance and patience, explored in Tool #18, *Stand Up and Know Your Needs*, centers on acceptance and patience for oneself, and is typified by the following saying in which I've always found a kernel of truth:

> *I'm perfect just as I am; and I could use a little improvement.*

Yes, we are perfectly imperfect beings—with ourselves and in our relationships. Acceptance and patience go a long way towards vanquishing the self-critical voices of shame, blame, and perfectionism. The following handout can help foster this practice.

TIPS FOR WORKING WITH CLIENTS

✓ The practice of forbearance is found in our wisdom traditions and fits nicely with the themes of acceptance and patience. Forbearance means that one makes a conscious choice to let something go. That is a true gift that one can offer a partner or others we care about.

✓ Make sure clients know they don't have to be perfect with acceptance and patience. Inviting inner hospitality while engaging in this process is the essence of self-acceptance and self-patience.

✓ For those wanting to cultivate an attitude and a practice of acceptance and patience, reinforce these qualities by bundling this tool with Tip #2, *Managing Expectations with a Mindful Model of Change*, Tool #15, *Accepting the Unwanted and Rejected*, Tool #23, *Grow Your Compassion Container*, and Tool #35, *The Gift of Forgiveness*.

Embracing Acceptance and Patience

Instructions

Acceptance and patience often go hand-in-hand. It's hard to think about having one without the other. These are attitudes that anyone can adopt and put into action. While there may be things you don't like or can't control in your life, you *can* control how you want to feel about it.

When it comes to fostering supportive relationships, the twin qualities of acceptance and patience can go a long way toward smoothing out or avoiding potential conflicts with those you care about. For example, having acceptance and patience doesn't mean that you necessarily agree with a particular situation or behavior. But what it *does* mean is that you can *choose* to be at peace with it. This is surrendering the I-centric viewpoint to something softer, kinder, and more open.

Use the following reflections to explore how you might bring acceptance and patience into your relationships and life.

Reflections

In the space below, write down an aspect of a relationship that you find difficult to accept and have patience for. This can be anything from a minor irritation to a major difference. What do you find most perplexing or challenging about this?

_____

_____

_____

Now, let's pretend for a moment that the situation was reversed. In other words, imagine switching places with the one you have difficulty with. Now that you are "standing in the other person's shoes," what does it feel like for you to be judged harshly or impatiently? Write down all the different emotions you might feel.

_____

_____

_____

Suppose you woke up in the morning and a miracle occurred so that you were fully accepting and patient with regards to the situation you identified above. How would you know this change really happened? What would be different in your speaking, actions, thinking, and feelings? How would this impact your relationship?

_____

_____

_____

What would it be like for you to make an executive decision to be more accepting and patient? Yes, you can decide to do that! Finally, how might this new attitude change your relationship? How might it benefit your health and well-being?

_____

_____

_____

Mental rehearsal is effective for helping athletes and others learn new behaviors. For 3–5 minutes, visualize yourself in the situation that provokes reactivity; only this time, picture yourself responding with dignity, grace, openness, and acceptance. As you visualize, relax your body, breathe slowly, and picture as many details as you can.

_____

_____

_____

Remember to be patient and accepting of yourself as you embrace these attitudes. Congratulations for moving in this new direction.

Tool #22 | Get C.U.R.I.O.U.S.

> ## Mindful Learning Styles
>
> The following learning styles are compatible with this curiosity tool:
>
> Verbal-Linguistic   Bodily-Kinesthetic-Tactile
>
> Visual-Spatial   Mathematical-Science-Logical
>
> Sound-Musical   Social-Interpersonal

THOUGHTS FOR THERAPISTS

"Isn't that interesting?" I gently queried with honest curiosity as the woman sitting in my office finished her painful telling of yet another seemingly unstoppable binge eating episode that left her in physical pain, demoralized, and filled with shame. We sat for some time in silence.

Then quietly I said, "Linda, what would it be like if you weren't critical about this binge, but instead got curious about what's going on?" Linda looked at me, doe-eyed and with more than a tinge of disbelief as I continued speaking. "The truth is that you were trying to take care of yourself by coping in the only way you knew in that moment. Let's be gentle and curious about this old behavior that isn't getting you what you want as an adult. Let's honor your tenacity and your will to live."

For a moment, think of a baby with its first pea, a toddler with its first spaghetti noodle—when do we lose the delight and adventure of curiosity? How can we help our clients reclaim that inquisitive, non-judgmental curiosity? In her work with students, the pioneering educator Maria Montessori harnessed curiosity. She believed it to be a core human trait that was critical to being an active and motivated participant in life and learning.

In another sense, curiosity can be viewed as the antidote and counterbalance to entrenched and rigid mindsets that try to control the show. Curiosity, for example, has been used in interventions for addiction and substance abuse. If someone gets curious about a craving or urge, that person *instantly develops a new relationship to it*. Instead of being caught in the all-or-none duality of resisting it or giving in to the craving, there's now a more compassionate and forgiving middle ground.

In the same way, curiosity is a powerful tool when applied to relationships. It lets us step out of old, fixed viewpoints; it helps us connect with others in an engaging way while sidestepping conflict.

TIPS FOR WORKING WITH CLIENTS

✓ At its essence, curiosity is about the mindfulness practice of learning how to take a non-judgmental stance. With this more spacious view, we can be more open and understanding of others.

✓ The following handout practice can be done with an individual or with partners.

✓ If someone likes to journal, it can be useful for clients to write down their "curiosity" experiences and how it changed their relationship to others.

✓ Consider combining this practice with Tool #14, *Mind Regulation for Making Peace with the Mind*, and Tool #21, *The Power of Acceptance and Patience*.

Get C.U.R.I.O.U.S.

Instructions

Do you remember the first time you saw a flower? A bird? A caterpillar? As a child, how wondrous and mysterious those simple things must have been! And yet as adults, it's easy to become oblivious to the many miraculous things that we pass by on a daily basis. It's as if a dark filter has drawn over our eyes and mind, blocking out the childlike curiosity that once filled us with joy.

What if you could remove the old filters and experience those who are in your life as if for the first time? Even that difficult person in your life (and we all have one or two) might be viewed very differently. This practice allows you to whole-heartedly participate and engage with others.

Use the steps in the acronym C.U.R.I.O.U.S.—individually, with a partner, or others—to transform ordinary awareness into one of curiosity. For Part 1, familiarize yourself with the acronym and then move on to Part 2.

PART 1 — *Get C.U.R.I.O.U.S.*

C — *Clean the Slate*

Clean your mental chalkboard of old beliefs, biases, and opinions. Imagine that you are a traveler, and that this is the first time you are meeting the person before you (partner, co-worker, friend, etc.). Mentally, picture yourself literally sweeping away (with a broom or your hands) old mindsets and pre-existing beliefs.

U — *Uniqueness*

See the uniqueness of the one before you. When you look into someone's eyes you are looking at someone with 100 billion neurons in the brain—and more connections between neurons than there are stars in the known universe! Tap this opportunity to spend even a few minutes with this most unique human in the universe.

R — *Revel in Excitement*

Like a traveler journeying in a new country, let yourself feel the excitement of discovery that accompanies curiosity. Don't be afraid to let your excitement show as you get curious.

I — *Inquire with Interest*

Genuine inquiry means you focus your curiosity and interest on the other person. Try to learn or discover as many novel things about this "new" exotic place or person. Inquire not from a critical, but an open, curious perspective. Even if you think you "know" this person, see how many new things you can learn.

O — *Opportunity to Learn*

Each interaction offers an opportunity to learn more, to get even more curious. Curiosity means you recognize that this moment is a precious gift that holds the potential for new memories.

U — *Understanding Without Judging*

With curiosity, you are not criticizing or judging another, but are just trying to get beneath the surface and understand. Curiosity doesn't mean changing or fixing what you're curious about. But it does mean you can deepen your understanding of the unique person before you.

S — *Share the Story*

What would you tell the people "back home" about the fascinating people and places you experienced on your travels? Just as there are different cultures with different traditions and ways of doing things, each person is like a mini-culture with his or her own history, tradition, and customs.

PART 2 — *C.U.R.I.O.U.S. Practice Guidelines*

1. Use a journal, mobile device, or an index card to keep track of your C.U.R.I.O.U.S. journeying experiences with others. To develop this practice, try to do this each day for the next week. You could even seek out people with very different viewpoints than your own and explore each as a new, unique culture.

2. If there's a relationship that feels stuck, try the acronym to step back from your habitual perspective and see if you can experience and understand this person in a fresh way.

3. Partners can use this practice together to get curious about one another. For example, two partners can explore areas—based on differing beliefs or behaviors—that are causing conflict. Each partner will take a turn getting C.U.R.I.O.U.S. with the other. When done, each can answer the questions below and compare notes on what they learned.

4. At the end of the week, look over your C.U.R.I.O.U.S. notes and writings and answer the following questions:

Reflections

Congratulations on this getting C.U.R.I.O.U.S. practice. What was it like to "clean your slate" of pre-conceived ideas and opinions before interacting with others? How did the thought of just getting curious shift your interactions?

_____

_____

_____

What was it like to look for something unique—even in someone you already know? What was the easiest thing about this? What was most challenging?

_____

_____

_____

What was your experience of "reveling in excitement"? How did this reconnect you with any childhood experiences of being curious? How did letting your excitement show affect the interaction?

_____

_____

_____

How different was it for you to "inquire with interest" rather than hold onto or promote your own point of view? How did this help you get more information?

_____

_____

_____

How did viewing this interaction as an "opportunity to learn" help you to have more patience and enjoy the moment?

_____

_____

_____

How did not taking a judgmental "right or wrong" stance help you to understand this other person better? What was it like to gain a new "understanding without judging" someone's story or past or experiences?

_____

_____

_____

Every traveler has fascinating stories to tell. What was it like to "share the story" of your unique journey of being curious with another?

_____

_____

_____

Tool #23 | # Grow Your Compassion Container

Mindful Learning Styles

This practice encourages individuals to find pleasantness that is around them by using the entire palette of learning styles:

- Verbal-Linguistic
- Visual-Spatial
- Sound-Musical
- Bodily-Kinesthetic-Tactile
- Mathematical-Science-Logical

- Social-Interpersonal
- Reflective-Intrapersonal
- Natural World
- Existential-Meaning

THOUGHTS FOR THERAPISTS

Perhaps one of the greatest magic tricks of all time is the illusion that each of us is distinct and separate from those around us. Sometimes that illusion is pierced, and the observer and the observed merge as one. These "one mind" experiences are frequent, whether we find ourselves thinking the same thing as a partner, knowing when something has happened to a loved one, or completely losing our sense of self while looking at nature's majesty, such as when peering down at the Grand Canyon.

Compassion—the ability to be with suffering—has the ability to dissolve the veil of separateness and reveal the truth behind the illusion. For example, I once had a client, Bill, who would get upset at his girlfriend's need for independence in their relationship. If she canceled or needed time to herself, Bill would stew and pout, experience self-doubt, and feel unloved. In other words, he strongly identified with his personal, egoistic needs. However, as Bill learned about compassion, he grasped how his suffering was coming from his own internal expectations of what he believed a relationship should be like. Rather than blame his girlfriend, he found empathy and a more caring and compassionate view of her situation. Through increased acceptance, compassion, understanding and patience, the relationship continued to grow in a natural way. You might say that Bill's compassion container got larger.

Paradoxically, growing our compassion container doesn't produce more suffering. On the contrary, it relieves and liberates us from unnecessary suffering. Like a gardener who pulls a weed out from its roots, so too can we alleviate suffering by recognizing its root causes. As discussed in Tip #1, *P.A.I.R. U.P. for Mindful Relationships*, a mindfulness-based relationship enhancement training for couples increased the ability to have compassion for one's partner. The handout for this tool provides one way of taking down the wall of protection that many have erected around the heart. With a compassion practice, that wall comes down slowly, bit by bit and brick by brick.

TIPS FOR WORKING WITH CLIENTS

✓ It's helpful for clients to recognize that suffering is produced as much by one's own inner perceptions and expectations as by what happens externally. In fact, more suffering is probably caused by non-acceptance of those conditions in life that are uncontrollable. Exploring the following ideas can be helpful:

- How has one's own attitudes contributed to suffering in the past?

- How has being attached to a particular outcome produced suffering?

- When someone understands her or his own role, or complicity, in suffering, it gives that person the ability to change thinking and behavior.

- By actively managing and working with life's difficult situations, one gains greater confidence and efficacy in these areas.

✓ How did one's family of origin deal with hardship? Was demonstrating compassion for others in the family a valued quality? To what extent did the client adopt the family's style of coping?

✓ Consider packaging together coping practices that include Tool #15, *Accepting the Unwanted and Rejected*, Tool #16, *Open the Compassionate Heart*, Tool #21, *The Power of Acceptance and Patience*, and Tool #38, *H.E.A.L. with Cooperative Listening*.

Grow Your Compassion Container

Instructions

The word "compassion" actually means *to be with suffering*. Usually, we think that our own suffering comes from things that happen to us. For example, you lose a job, you fall and break your leg, or you get divorced. It's easy to point at those situations as what cause pain. And yes, while those events are the initial cause of suffering, there is often a second and even more powerful kind of suffering that tags along for the ride. And that is *the story of how you hate what has happened to you.*

For example, yes, I broke my leg and am now in a cast—that is one kind of suffering. Now, the second suffering that is *optional and added on* is my reaction and rejection of the experience. That story might be, "I hate that I broke my leg because it shouldn't have happened. I'm angry and upset that I can't ride my bike now, and that I'm stuck indoors. And I don't like how people look at me when I'm in a wheelchair or use crutches." A deeper understanding of what is causing suffering can help you defuse it.

If you have had a disagreement or argument with a significant person in your life, spend a few minutes reflecting using Part 1, before sitting with that person in Part 2 of this practice. Ideally, both persons would use the handout here to grow their compassion containers.

PART 1 — *Reflections*

What happened that is causing you to suffer right now? Write down the actual "event" that happened (the initial suffering). Then, write down the "story" you have about this and how it makes you react and feel (the second suffering).

_____

_____

_____

How much of your "story" involves your expectations about how things or another person "should be"? To what extent are your expectations or beliefs contributing to this story of added-on suffering?

_____

_____

_____

What would it be like to let go of the "story" for even a few minutes? Might there be another way of understanding why another person acted as they did? If you were in that other person's shoes, why might you have acted in this way?

_____

_____

_____

PART 2 — *Sitting with Compassionate Presence*

Everyone has a "difficult" person in their life—someone who knows exactly which of your buttons to push. What would it be like, however, if you could set aside your assumptions about this difficult person? What if you could view them with a fresh perspective? That's what a compassion practice like this one can help you to do.

Before starting this practice, read the following anecdotal story of a reporter who goes to Africa to interview a tribal leader.

> *After a long and arduous trek through the African wilderness, a reporter finally arrives at the village where he has come to interview a well-known tribal leader. When the journalist meets with the translator, he is told about a unique custom. According to the custom, the reporter must first sit in silence with the tribal leader before asking any questions. The reporter agrees so he can get his story.*
>
> *The reporter sits opposite the tribal leader, and they look directly at one another without speaking. The journalist finds this awkward for the first five minutes, but expects it to end soon. But after 20 minutes have gone by, the reporter's mind frantically thinks, "When is this going to end?!" After 30 minutes go by, and then 50 minutes, the reporter finally gives up trying to guess, and finally lets go of fighting the experience. He breathes easily as he gazes into the tribal leader's eyes. After over an hour has passed, the reporter has lost all track of time… even track of himself! For a time, the reporter has the feeling that looking at the tribal leader is like looking in a mirror. It's as if a deep understanding, or communion, has taken place between himself and tribal leader.*
>
> *Finally, the tribal leader nods at the journalist, as if to say, "we are finished." The leader's translator looks at the reporter and says, "You can now ask your questions."*
>
> *"Tell your leader 'thank you' but I have no questions. I've learned everything I need to know about him just by sitting here with him in silence!"*

For the next three minutes, you will sit in silence with another. As you sit, you will be sitting with a compassionate gaze and presence. What this means is that you will focus on the suffering that you and this other person share. All humans endure loss, sadness, grief, and aging. This is part of being human, and it is part of the richness of our shared human experience. No one can escape or avoid these conditions of life. In addition, this practice offers the opportunity to notice the uniqueness of the person before you. Each of us—with more neural connections than there are stars in the known universe(!)—is the most unique person in the entire universe.

As you begin, remember this:

No one owns or purchases the future. All anyone can really count on is this thin sliver of time and space called *now*. Why not appreciate and honor the one who inhabits it with you?

Even if you notice awkwardness, that's okay. Just breathe and be present in a compassionate way with the one before you. Each partner will complete the following reflections and then share them.

Reflections

What did it feel like to sit with another for three minutes in this way?

_____

_____

_____

What was most challenging about sitting in this way? What was easiest or satisfying about sitting with another in this way?

_____

_____

_____

What new understanding do you have about this person and their life? What is one deeper understanding this can give you in times of disagreement or conflict?

_____

_____

_____

Tool #24 | # S.T.O.P. the Relationship Robot of Reactivity

Mindful Learning Styles

This multi-purpose practice encompasses all nine learning styles:

- Verbal-Linguistic
- Visual-Spatial
- Sound-Musical
- Bodily-Kinesthetic-Tactile
- Mathematical-Science-Logical

- Social-Interpersonal
- Reflective-Intrapersonal
- Natural World
- Existential-Meaning

THOUGHTS FOR THERAPISTS

Each of us has a robot inside that is more than willing to take over. The robot works on autopilot, which means it can quickly circumvent the thinking brain and run a pre-installed software program. There are advantages to this in some cases. When driving your car, for example, procedural memory takes over. After all, you don't want to have to learn how to drive all over again! But there are many times when the robot takes over, thus robbing us of our free will and purposeful choice. When this happens, entrenched and often toxic ways of thinking, acting, and feeling can take over.

The robot can easily hijack our relationships, too, setting in motion a habitual cycle of negativity and reactivity. Fortunately, brain science shows that we can pause automatic negative mental programs before they start. That's because, according to the research of neuroscientist Benjamin Libet, each of us possesses *free won't*, which is the equally powerful flip side of *free will*. In *Mind Time*, Libet wrote, "The existence of a veto possibility is not in doubt. The subjects in our experiments at times reported that conscious wish or urge to act appeared but that they suppressed or vetoed it."[21]

The handout activates *free won't* veto power. One important point to make is that each time someone exercises veto power, the intentional circuitry of the brain is engaged and strengthened. Conversely, the impulsive, autopilot programming is weakened. This gives anyone the ability to pause, or in this case, to S.T.O.P. and turn in a new and more beneficial direction.

While a similar practice was included in *The Mindfulness Toolbox*, this one is very different because it is applied specifically to working with relationship triggers.

---

[21] Benjamin Libet, *Mind Time* (Cambridge, MA: Harvard University Press, 2005), p. 141.

TIPS FOR WORKING WITH CLIENTS

✓ Demonstrate the S.T.O.P. practice in your office the first time, as clients follow along. This can be done with individuals or partners, using the handout as a guided script. Then, provide a handout for practicing. It also helps to first identify the following for helping to clarify when and how to use the practice.

- Identify those relationship triggers and patterns that keep repeating.

- Establish in advance how and when to best utilize this tool.

- Decide how this will work, such as taking a twenty-minute break and finding separate areas for practicing S.T.O.P.

- Establish a routine for coming back together after the practice. What would this look like? What could be discussed?

✓ When working with automatic or toxic behaviors, repetition is very important in changing these patterns. For that reason, consider the following:

- Have clients practice the handout S.T.O.P. practice for 15–30 minutes at a time for several days.

- Have clients schedule practice sessions for the week.

- It may help to write down the S.T.O.P. practice steps into the notes of a cell phone or on an index card. Refer to this as needed.

✓ Preparation for this practice is the overall Mindfulness Body/Breath/Mind Meditation covered in Tools #12, #13, and #14. Bundle this handout with the following practices for going off autopilot and being more intentional—Tool #25, *Using Affirmations as a Relationship GPS*, and Tool #29, *Rituals for Coming and Going.*

S.T.O.P. the Relationship Robot of Reactivity

Instructions

Did you ever get sleepy behind the wheel of your car? When that happens, you lose control of the steering wheel and the car drifts dangerously. Similarly, whenever an old habit takes hold, it's like being asleep at the wheel. You are no longer really in control because the embedded habit—which runs a mindless, automatic program in your mind—takes over.

This practice gets your hands back on the steering wheel so you can turn in the direction you want. It can help you pause and reset when an old relationship pattern—or any toxic behavior—starts to put you in automatic mode. And because this practice is portable, you can use it almost anytime and anywhere.

Follow along with the acronym S.T.O.P. Each of the letters stands for the four steps that will give you the ability to slow down, calm yourself, recognize your emotions, and then get off autopilot and move in a positive direction. Anytime you feel yourself getting upset or triggered, separate and give yourself distance from a partner. Then, in a quiet space reset by using S.T.O.P.

S — *Stop, Stand & Breathe*

This first step is important because it actually quiets down the reactive part of the brain that triggers the fight and flight response. Once the stress response kicks in, you stop listening and get defensive. Don't blame yourself—this happens to everyone. What you can do right now is **stand with your hands clasped behind your back and breathe deeply into the belly.** (Refer to Tool #20, *Self-Soothing and Synchronized Breathing*, for information on diaphragmatic breathing.) Take three to five belly breaths. This will turn on the body's relaxation response. It also helps bring your thinking brain back online!

T — *Tune In to the Body*

Starting from the bottom of the feet, scan upwards into the legs, the torso, the internal organs, the chest and back, the hands and arms, all the way up to the head. **Notice where there is any tightness or tension in the body, and name whatever emotions you are feeling.**

Naming emotions quiets down the emotional part of the brain because instead of reacting to the emotion, you are changing your relationship to it—and using the thinking brain to observe and process it. *Try to name as many emotions as you can*—even the deeper emotions. For example, you might be angry, but beneath the anger you may feel hurt, sad, and disappointed. All of these can exist together. Knowing and naming the deeper emotions can give you greater understanding—and a more complete and articulate way of describing your feelings to your partner.

Finally, imagine taking an in-breath and breathe into the tension, tightness, or emotion. As you exhale, imagine the breath carrying that tension or negative emotion down the body and out the bottom of the feet and back into the earth for recycling.

O — *Observe Pleasantness*

Now that you've calmed the body and worked with releasing your emotions, you will bring your awareness to your surroundings. **Here, notice one pleasant thing around you—a sound, a color, an object, or a shape.** This will soothe you by focusing on something pleasant, such as your favorite color, the chirping of a bird, or an object you like. Let yourself enjoy that soothing thing for a few moments.

P — *Positive Preparation*

Now that you've paused and regulated yourself—both inwardly and with the external environment—you are no longer on autopilot or reactive. You are ready to prepare for the next helpful action. **What is the next positive or beneficial action you want to take on behalf of yourself and the relationship?** That could be anything from listening to soothing music to talking with a friend or counselor. You might think about what action could help to repair the relationship in this moment. You may also want to consider examining Tool #25, *Using Affirmations as a Relationship GPS*—using this as a guide to ensure that your next action aligns with your values.

You could also reflect on what happened—such as looking at how going on autopilot has affected you in the past and how you want to change that behavior. You may want to share your feelings with someone close and trusted. What's important is that you stay calm as you move forward. Consider exploring Tool #22, *Get C.U.R.I.O.U.S.*

Reflections

What was it like to practice the S.T.O.P. practice? What was most difficult about it? What was easiest?

_____

_____

_____

How will you initiate this practice when you need it? How do you think you can best put this into practice?

_____

_____

_____

Like any skill, this one requires a lot of practice to perfect it—such as 15–30 minutes at a time, from three to five times a week for a couple of weeks. That way, when you need it, it will come naturally. What would a practice schedule look like for you? How can you create a plan and put it into effect? If you are doing this with another, you can practice together.

_____

_____

_____

Tool #25 | # Using Affirmations as a Relationship GPS

Mindful Learning Styles

This practice fits nicely with the following ways of getting present:

Verbal-Linguistic   Social-Interpersonal

Visual-Spatial   Reflective-Intrapersonal

Sound-Musical   Existential-Meaning

Mathematical-Science-Logical

THOUGHTS FOR THERAPISTS

Mindfulness is very much about intentionality and awareness of thoughts and choices. As demonstrated in the previous Tool #24, *S. T.O.P. the Relationship Robot of Reactivity*, intentionality assists us in slowing down so as to make conscious choices about what to do next. In relationships, intentionality is put to work for the betterment of the relationship—so both partners have a clear roadmap for knowing how to protect and safeguard the relationship. In this sense, intention acts like a GPS that lets partners know if they're moving in the right direction or whether they are lost and off course.

One useful way of setting intentions is through shared affirmations. Affirmations are positively-oriented statements that focus attention and prime the brain for action. According to psychiatrist Daniel Siegel, "Intention is a central organizing process in the brain that creates continuity beyond the present moment."[22] Relationships that lack core values, or affirmations, can easily get lost or sidetracked. Even the Navy SEALS, for example, teach their recruits to use affirmations, or positive self-talk, in order to get them through their difficult training.

Affirmations that describe deeper values are relevant because they literally shape and define our relationships. Former monk Thomas Moore affirmed this idea in *Soul Mates* when he wrote, "From the point of view of soul, identity is not a solitary achievement but a communal experience, always implying a relationship to others."[23] But how do we put this into action? The handout here is a guide to creating strong, positive, and pro-active affirmations for relationships.

TIPS FOR WORKING WITH CLIENTS

✓ Exploring a client's past history might reveal the values or beliefs that existed in one's family of origin.

---

[22] Daniel Siegel, *The Mindful Brain* (New York: W. W. Norton & Company, 2007), p. 177.
[23] Thomas Moore, *Soul Mates* (New York: Harper Perennial, 1994), p. 105.

✓ This value setting can be done individually, with a partner, or in groups. Parents, for example, could use this to clarify values for their marriage or parenting.

✓ Consider bundling this practice with the following:

- Tool #16, *Open the Compassionate Heart*
- Tool #20, *Self-Soothing and Synchronized Breathing*
- Tool #23, *Grow Your Compassion Container*

✓ **Note:** The handout/practice that follows can also be used in conjunction with the *Creating a Personal Intention Statement* handout found in *The Mindfulness Toolbox*. These are complementary handouts for developing values for family, parenting, career, etc.

Using Affirmations as a Relationship GPS

Instructions

Relationships often thrive or wither depending on the deeper values, or affirmations, that support them. You can think of affirmations as being like a GPS or navigation program in your car. Not only do they keep you from getting lost and off course, best of all they can help you safely find the way back *"home."*

Affirmations are one way of being intentional that primes your brain and body. Affirmations get us ready and prepared to move and act. We need them to keep us focused on doing the things that matter to us—such as getting exercise or eating nutritiously—otherwise it's easy to get sidetracked, distracted, affected by stress, and so on.

For this practice, you will begin with a meta-affirmation—a deeper value that reflects a guiding principle for how you want to express and safeguard your relationship. For example, the meta-affirmation of *"being a respectful partner"* would be expressed on a daily basis through numerous actions, such as speaking respectfully, being honest, and not interrupting, among others. Follow along with the practice below to get familiar with affirmations.

Step 1 — *Meta-Affirmations Are a Choice*

Meta-affirmations are most effective when stated positively, as something you actively *choose* to have in your life—as opposed to thinking of what you don't want in your life. For example, rather than saying *"I don't want a relationship where there is dishonesty and mistrust,"* it's better to state that idea in positive terms. That might look like: *"Each day, I choose to cultivate a relationship that is honest and trusting."*

Remember to add the words *"I choose* or *We choose"* to your relationship affirmation.

Step 2 — *Meta-Affirmations Are Not Specific Goals, but Guiding Principles*

The meta-affirmation is a larger statement of what you want to manifest in your relationship. The goals will follow as specific actions that support this meta-affirmation. Let's say your overall affirmation is: *"I (we) choose to have a relationship based on transparency and honesty"*. The actual actions that support this could be such things as checking in via phone or text or email during the day, as well as letting your partner have access to your phone and email. Those daily actions are the observable and measurable goals that can be written down after creating the meta-affirmation.

Step 3 — *Write a Meta-Affirmation for Your Relationship*

You can have several meta-affirmations for your relationship. Look over the words below—these are just a few suggestions—or use your own words to create a single meta-affirmation, or value that you want as a guiding principle in your relationship.

"Loving, Trusting, Respectful, Joyful, Physically Healthy, Honest, Forgiving, Loyal, Reliable, Generous, etc."

You can also combine several ideas together, such as: "*I (we) choose to create a mutually loving relationship that includes the values of loyalty, patience, generosity, openness, forgiveness, steadfastness, and forbearance.*"

Every relationship is unique in knowing what matters to the partners or individuals involved. Take some time to craft a positively stated, affirmative choice in the space below:

_____

_____

_____

_____

Step 4 — *Write Observable Actions that Support Your Meta-Affirmation*

To put the meta-affirmation into action, you need observable and sustainable behaviors that let you know it's working. What actions tell you that the deeper values are being supported? Write these below.

_____

_____

_____

_____

Reflections

What was it like for you to create a meta-affirmation? What was the most challenging thing about it? What was the easiest? Creating affirmations is a process, and you will have the opportunity to go back and refine them.

_____

_____

_____

_____

What was it like to come up with supporting behaviors and actions? How will you know if these need to be changed? Carry your meta-affirmation with you and look at it daily. Keeping it in mind is one way to keep your Relationship GPS working!

_____

_____

_____

_____

Tool #26 | # Enhance Relationships with a Positive Shared Memory

---

Mindful Learning Styles

The following learning styles are compatible with this shared memory practice:

Verbal-Linguistic   Social-Interpersonal

Visual-Spatial   Reflective-Intrapersonal

Sound-Musical   Existential-Meaning

The brain is very much wired by where we place our attention. Research shows that focusing on memories or past experiences can affect how we feel. The positive psychology field, for example, has been studying what is called "savoring," or the practice of deliberately focusing on warm memories, accomplishments, and past successes. Perhaps it is not surprising that by re-experiencing positive memories we can enhance positive affect and self-esteem. But what would happen if we shared our positive stories with another?

As published in the *Journal of Social and Personal Relationships*, researchers conducted a series of studies that examined the effects of sharing a positive memory.[24] Researchers found that focusing on positive memory—such as keeping a gratitude journal—increased positive affect. The act of sharing that experience with another gave an additional boost to one's sense of well-being. Further, researchers found that one practice in particular produced the highest levels of happiness, life satisfaction, and positive emotions. That happened when people who shared their stories got what was termed "active-constructive" feedback to the story. In other words, it was the interaction and positive response from a partner that was most satisfying and effective.

Mindfulness promotes a willing openness to all of life's experiences—the good, the bad, and the indifferent. It's worth noting that this practice does not invalidate or ignore the fact that difficult life experiences are laden with meaning and growth potential. But there are times when dwelling on the past negatives—especially in a relationship—unfairly focuses on one side of life experiences. Noticing and sharing the positive is a nurturing practice intended to nourish and grow relationships with the balance they deserve.

---

[24] Nathaniel Lambert, A. Marlea Gwinn, et al., A boost of positive affect: The perks of sharing positive experiences, *Journal of Social and Personal Relationships*, 2012: 1–20.

TIPS FOR WORKING WITH CLIENTS

✓ Have clients practice sharing a positive memory in session. Each person gets a turn to share a meaningful memory and get feedback.

- Each person will think of a positive story in which both participated.

✓ The practice of sharing a positive memory is a flexible one. Longtime partners, for example, may like sharing significant events of tranquility and contentment.

- Each person can focus on a shared story of an experience that reflects a well-lived life.

✓ Try using the *Enhance Relationships with a Positive Shared Memory* handout with these complementary tools:

- Tool #25, *Using Affirmations as a Relationship GPS*
- Tool #27, *Identifying Strengths to Build Closeness*
- Tool #28, *The Tenderness of Touch and Intimacy*

Enhance Relationships with a Positive Shared Memory

Instructions

Just as focusing on something negative can "bring you down," focusing on a positive event in your life can lift up your mood. Any relationship—at work or at home—can benefit from sharing and savoring positive memories together. Even if things are difficult in the moment, sharing good times from the past is like getting a positive booster vaccination. This might help you remember, for example, how you and another worked together to accomplish something or just have fun. So right now, get ready to recognize the positive times that you can appreciate together.

Go through the following steps one person at a time. This way each will get a chance to both share a story and respond to the partner's story.

Note: If appropriate and it feels right, ask if you can hold the listener's hand while sharing the story. Consider using Tool #28, *The Tenderness of Touch and Intimacy*, before this exercise as a way to experience physiological alignment and coherence.

1. Identify a Positive Story—An Experience Shared by Both Persons

Think about a positive memory from the past that you experienced with another, such as a partner, family member, friend, or other. This can be an experience that fostered a sense of togetherness, brought a sense of shared success or accomplishment, or was unique, meaningful, joyful, or memorable in some way. Write down the event and include the highlights of what stands out for you.

As you recall this positive memory, pay attention to how it feels in the body.

_____

_____

_____

_____

_____

_____

_____

_____

_____

_____

_____

2. Share the Story with a Partner (Who Listens with Empathy)

As you share this story, include as many details as you can—sights, sounds, smells, etc. Remember to point out not just *what* happened, but *the positive emotions of how it felt—such as exciting, exhilarating, joyful, adventurous, romantic, etc*. The emotional side of the story is important. The listener does not respond or interrupt at this time, but *just listens and re-experiences the story through hearing it*.

3. The Listener Responds and Shares Personal Recollections

After hearing the story, the listener will now share what it was like to hear this story by answering the following questions:

- What emotions did the listener feel when hearing this story?
- What are this listener's own recollections of the story?
- What did the listener like most about how the story was shared and told?

4. Partners Discuss What This Story Means for Them

Partners can write down and then discuss, or just discuss what a story like the one they just shared says about them. What relationship strengths does the story reveal? What relationship skills? What kind of trust?

_____

_____

_____

_____

Are these strengths and activities part of the present-day relationship? If not, how can they be regained or incorporated?

_____

_____

_____

_____

Lastly, after concluding this exercise, the above steps are repeated by reversing the roles. The listener is now the one telling a shared experience.

Tool #27 | # Identifying Strengths to Build Closeness

Mindful Learning Styles

The following are compatible with this practice of identifying another's strengths:

Verbal-Linguistic

Visual-Spatial

Sound-Musical

Bodily-Kinesthetic-Tactile

Mathematical-Science-Logical

Social-Interpersonal

Reflective-Intrapersonal

Natural World

Existential-Meaning

THOUGHTS FOR THERAPISTS

The idea of identifying strengths has been in all of my books because I believe it's fundamental to accurately portraying all the different coping skills we use on a daily basis. And yet, it's easy to diminish or devalue the idea of noticing one's own strengths—as if it's a phony, ego-centered practice. But to purposely avoid looking at strengths is to deny the truth of how many different abilities are necessary to survive in our complex world.

In workshops, I like to point out that when people wake up in the morning, get showered, brush their teeth, and eat breakfast, they are engaging several important self-care strengths. The simple act of getting dressed, for example, requires the strengths of decision-making and planning in order to find the proper clothing that fits with the current weather conditions—not to mention the strengths of follow-through and action. Other commonplace and frequently ignored strengths include making it to work or any appointment on time (strengths of discipline and organization), walking the dog (strengths of compassion and caring), and making breakfast or lunch for family members (strengths of planning, hospitality, and responsibility). In fact, the next time you park at the mall, you might appreciate that the miracle of locating your car in that gigantic parking lot is made possible through the strength of memory!

Research from psychologist Martin Seligman and others has shown that a simple strengths practice—such as identifying one's strength and putting it in to action once a day—can significantly reduce symptoms of depression.[25] More than that, noticing strengths helps us recognize our coping skills and the coping skills of others. Most importantly, it offers real evidence that partners are not taking one another for granted.

---

[25] M.E.P. Selgiman, T. Rashid, & A.C. Parks, Positive psychotherapy, *The American Psychologist*, 2006, Nov; 61(8): 774–788.

TIPS FOR WORKING WITH CLIENTS

✓ Use the handout that follows as a guided script, and read this to clients before they practice telling their stories and identifying strengths.

✓ Some individuals discount strengths as being routine or just "what I do."

✓ When strengths are rejected as a concept, offering research might help, as well as an exploration of family history around how personal strengths were viewed.

✓ An unintended benefit of a strengths practice is that it changes how partners listen to one another. They learn how to listen for the strengths instead of listening for the complaint or preparing to get defensive.

✓ Two helpful resources include my book *101 Mindful Ways to Build Resilience*, which is filled with many practical and easy-to-use strength-oriented exercises and concepts, and the VIA-IS online strengths questionnaire. This free assessment takes only 15 minutes and identifies 24 core strengths.

  • http://www.viacharacter.org

Identifying Strengths to Build Closeness

How did you cope today? Everyone has to get through the day using many coping skills. Driving through rush hour traffic, for example, requires many skills: attention, awareness of surroundings, spatial and distance skills, and a good sense of direction. And by the way, having good reflexes sure helps! Then, there is a whole other set of coping skills you use in the workplace. Yes, all these can be thought of as coping skills—but in another sense, they represent your strengths. Strengths are personal qualities that help you to effectively problem-solve obstacles that you face each day.

For example, when you brush your teeth and take a shower each morning you are using strengths of self-care and discipline. When you call on someone at home or the office to help you out with something, you are using the strengths of relationships and locating resources. When you volunteer to help out someone at work you are engaging the strengths of generosity, hospitality, and compassion. If you can laugh at your own foibles and the stresses you face, you are using the strengths of humor and self-knowing awareness. Even finding your car in that giant mall parking lot is the strength of memory!

One organization has assembled over 100 character strengths. You can take a free 15-minute assessment and identify your top 24 core strengths at viacharacter.org. Looking at a list of strengths before doing this exercise is not necessary, but it may give you more ideas about the many kinds of strengths you already possess.

Instructions

Read this introduction for how to listen and how to tell the story before beginning.

For this practice one person is going to share a simple story with his or her partner—such as going to the store, what happened at work during the day, or taking care of some other apparently ordinary daily chore or business.

1. **The Story Teller Includes the Six Following Details in the Story**
   - **History**
     - This means digging deeper into one's previous experience and feelings about doing a particular job, task, or activity. For example, if you had to get on the freeway or deal with rush hour traffic as part of your story, what is your "history" around that? How do you manage to cope with it? Do you try to avoid the traffic, find a new route, or wait until it dies down?
     - Maybe you have a history around dealing with a particular person, task, or going into a particular store. Make sure you include this.
   - **Stressors**
     - Some stressors are related to getting enough sleep and enough to eat, which affects the ability to function. Other stressors include time constraints, family, and other obligations. And again, how did you manage to cope with these stressors?

- **Moods and Thoughts**
  - No one stands in the same river of moods and thoughts for very long. When you woke up in the morning, did you have a mental "to-do" list and anxious thoughts running in your head? How did you work around these mental and emotional obstacles?

- **The Body**
  - The body has a story and an influence of its own. For example, were you able to take care of the body—such as finding time for stretching, walking, or exercising? Did the body have issues that affected you adversely? How did you cope in spite of these issues?

- **Habits**
  - What habits did you engage in that either helped or hindered your ability to attain your goal? Some habits, like getting out of bed the moment you hear the alarm, might have helped you. Others, like not paying attention to the time, might have produced a different result.

- **Centering Rituals**
  - What things did you do that helped you get through the day and made things a little easier for you? Did the clothing you picked out have a comforting texture or cheerful color that soothed you? Did you purposely choose to put on certain music during your transition in the car? Maybe a hot cup of coffee helped you feel more comforted, centered, and focused for the day ahead? Think of all the ways you helped yourself center so you could attain your goals.

2. The Listener Reflects Back the Identified Strengths

The listener has a very special job. You are listening, but not in the usual way. The listener's role is to identify the strengths that are in the story. Do not interrupt, but listen with interest and empathy through the entire story. When the story is over, you will share, or reflect back as many strengths as you found in the story. If it helps you to write these on a notepad as you're listening that's okay.

3. The Story Teller Expresses What It Was Like to Hear His or Her Own Strengths

The real secret here is to let the strengths in. If it helps, pretend you are listening about the strengths of someone else. Appreciate the strengths that you possess. After you hear your strengths, tell your partner what it was like for you to hear these. Was it surprising? Affirming? Satisfying?

Afterwards, the roles are reversed and the Story Teller takes the role of the Listener, and vice versa.

Reflections

Now you and your partner have had the chance to share a story and listen for strengths, let's explore this a little further. What was it like to *listen* for strengths? How different was this than your normal way of listening? What was the easiest thing about it? What was most challenging?

_____

_____

_____

_____

What was it like to hear your strengths reflected back to you? How did it feel to know that someone understood and appreciated your strengths? How are your strengths and those of your partner similar? How are they complementary?

_____

_____

_____

_____

_____

_____

A Weekly Strengths Practice

As a practice, notice one of your partner's strengths each day and then share that with your partner.

Another practice is to put one of your own strengths into action once a day for a week in a way that supports your partner. Each person can write down these experiences and at the end of a week, compare notes on sharing your strengths with one another.

Tool #28	# The Tenderness of Touch and Intimacy

Mindful Learning Styles

The following learning styles are compatible with this practice:

Verbal-Linguistic   Social-Interpersonal

Visual-Spatial   Existential-Meaning

Bodily-Kinesthetic-Tactile

THOUGHTS FOR THERAPISTS

We've all experienced being in the presence of someone who embodied a deep state of being calm, stable, and peaceful. Likely, that apparently unreactive person was experiencing a state of being in the zone—which can be thought of as experiencing physiological and psychological coherence. Researchers are exploring how a coherent state might be transmitted to others—such as through touch. Before examining how this can apply to relationships, let's investigate coherence. Coherence, for example, has different meanings depending on the context—such as physics or physiology. In a mindfulness context, coherence essentially means that body and mind are in a state of integration, wholeness, receptivity, and availability to others.

Even the heart reaches a coherent state, which is necessary for producing greater harmony and integration between the body's many subsystems. Research conducted by the Institute of HeartMath has shown that positive emotions actually generate greater rhythmic coherence in the heart. In addition, the heart produces an electromagnetic field that is more pronounced than any other part of the body, including the brain. This matters for relationships because touch plays an important energetic role in sharing information—even transmitting heart signals between two persons holding hands.[26]

We have long known, for example, that individuals who feel empathy for their partner while talking about even difficult topics have matching heart rates.[27] In this sense, we can see that intimacy is about developing and building coherence with those around us.

This integration with another is transformative, as described by Paul Eluard when he wrote:

> *I can understand another soul only by transforming my own,*
> *as one person transforms his hand by placing it in another's.*[28]

[26] Rollin McCraty, Ph.D., *The Energetic Heart: Bioelectromagnetic Interactions Within and Between People* (Boulder Creek, CA: HeartMath Institute, 2003).

[27] Robert W. Levenson and Anna M. Ruef, Physiological Aspects of Emotional Knowledge and Rapport. W. Ickes, editor. *Empathic Accuracy* (New York: Guilford Press, 1997).

[28] David Richo, *How to Be an Adult in Relationships* (Boston, MA: Shambhala, 2002), p. 228.

TIPS FOR WORKING WITH CLIENTS

What is a client's history around touch? It's important for clients to recognize that intimacy is not necessarily sexual in nature. Intimacy means closeness and deep connection. Touch through a hug or a kind pat on the shoulder can build intimacy and trust.

✓ If there's trauma, this needs to be addressed first. What kind of touch is appropriate? What would healing or helping touch look like?

✓ To find additional resources on building intimacy and resilience through movement, a useful source is the American Dance Therapy Association website.

• adta.org

✓ Other tools that can be used along with this one include body awareness Tool #17, *Sensing and Honoring the Body*, and Tool #26, *Enhance Relationships with a Positive Shared Memory*.

Attuning with Touch and Intimacy

Touch and movement are the most fundamental ways that we connect and build trust with others. The first thing we experience as babies is being held closely. Think for a moment about a kind hug or pat on the shoulder that made you feel good. Used in the right way, touch builds intimacy and safety, as well as gives us a sense of reciprocity. The following practice will let you explore touch as you establish closeness with another.

PART 1 — *Mirroring*

Instructions

Stand opposite each other at a comfortable distance. Have one person go first and make slow movements as the second person mirrors, or mimics, these movements. This movement might be swaying to-and-fro, walking, moving the arms and hands, or even making facial expressions. The idea is to mirror whatever movements the partner makes.

After doing this for about three minutes, stop and reverse roles.

Now the second person will lead the movement as the other person follows, or mirrors, the movements for another three minutes. When done, both persons will reflect on the following:

Reflections

What did it feel like to follow along and "mirror" your partner? What did it feel like for the person who was initiating or leading the movement?

_____

_____

_____

_____

How well synchronized were you both? Does this remind you of any other time when you have felt in sync with one another?

_____

_____

_____

_____

How could mirroring help you get more connected with one another during the typical day?

_____

_____

_____

_____

PART 2 — *Co-Balancing*

Instructions

Stand opposite the other person at a comfortable distance. Both persons will raise their arms until palms are facing outward at chest height. Slowly, the partners will move their palms closer until they notice even the most subtle sensation of heat, warmth, energy, or pressure. Stop and just notice what this is like.

Then, slowly continue to move the palms and hands closer until just the fingertips of your hands touch the fingertips of your partner's hands. This is a very light, gentle touch. Notice if you can feel the other person's pulse, which can sometimes be felt as a tingling in the fingertips.

Next, very slowly bring the hands closer until the palms gently touch. As you do this, however, notice which parts of the hands come into contact *before* the palms touch. How do the fingers straighten out? How does the positioning of the wrists change ever so slightly?

Now that the hands are touching, notice the feeling between your palms and the palms of your partner. Is more heat building up? Stand this way for up to a minute, just sensing.

Next, reach out with both arms and hands, and hold your partner firmly above the wrist. You are now connected and supporting one another. As you do this, plant your feet solidly and begin to sway gently back and forth, like a seesaw. As one moves back, the other person acts as a counterbalance, supporting the other. This takes some practice, and you may find that bending your knees gives you more leverage. Don't pull hard; this is not a contest or competition, but a supportive and cooperative stance. The idea is to make your partner feel safe and protected, even as they might lean back slightly. You don't have to lean back very far; even a few inches is enough as long as your partner counterbalances and helps you feel safe and secure.

Do this for about three minutes. Then, gently release each other's arms.

Reflections

What did it feel like to gently touch your partner's palms? Did you feel energy between the palms even before they touched?

_____

_____

_____

_____

How did sensing each other's palms enhance a sense of closeness or safety?

_____

_____

_____

_____

What did it feel like to be supported, or held, by your partner while see-sawing or moving back and forth? What would it be like for you to have this feeling of support in other areas of your life?

_____

_____

_____

_____

What would it be like to use this co-balancing practice after a disagreement? How could you use this practice to just feel reconnected?

_____

_____

_____

_____

Tool #29 | Rituals for Coming and Going

Mindful Learning Styles

The following learning styles are compatible with this practice:

Verbal-Linguistic   Bodily-Kinesthetic-Tactile

Sound-Musical   Social-Interpersonal

THOUGHTS FOR THERAPISTS

Have you ever heard of the term *phubbing*? It's a word formed by combining the "ph" from the word *phone* with the "ubbing" from the word *snubbing*. So when someone you're talking to checks their phone and isn't paying attention, they are *phubbing* you. Getting *phubbed* doesn't have a good sound to it, does it? One study looked at how technology affected the relationships of couples and found that the implicit messages sent out to partners by *phubbing* negatively affected relationships and even produced conflict.[29]

The point here is not just how we are *with* others, but how are we with them *during those all-important coming and going moments*. These are important moments because they determine how we securely attach with those we are close to. Leaving is about *closure and connection*. Wishing someone a "nice day," along with a wave, hug, or kiss, provides a sense of meaningful closure. Leaving also requires a ritual for connection, which means sharing how you will stay in touch later. That might be letting your friend, partner, or other person know how you will stay in touch—such as through text, email, or phone. Or, you might let them know when you safely arrive at your destination. When you think about it, even going to sleep is a form of leaving the awake, conscious world that requires an attachment ritual for closure and connection.

Likewise, when we return home or enter a space, it's helpful to feel safe and included. Such ritual behaviors as giving a big smile, a hug, and asking, "How was your day?" can accomplish this. But if someone is at the computer when you return home and doesn't bother to look up when you come home, it's hard to feel safe, welcomed, and included. Even in the workplace, being positively greeted when entering or leaving are important rituals to set in place.

At their core, these leaving and entering rituals help to reduce anxiety and promote closeness. In the handout that follows, partners will learn how to recognize and install small rituals that produce big results.

---

[29] Brandon McDaniel and Sarah Coyne, "Technoference": The Interference of Technology in Couple Relationships and Implications for Women's Personal and Relational Well-Being, DOI: 10.1037/ppm0000065, https://www.researchgate.net/publication/269334974_Technoference_The_Interference_of_Technology_in_Couple_Relationships_and_Implications_for_Women's_Personal_and_Relational_Well-Being (Accessed April, 2017).

TIPS FOR WORKING WITH CLIENTS

✓ It can be helpful to explore what rituals are already in place for coming and going in the relationship.

✓ Do a short "technology intake" to see how each person uses technology. Is it intrusive or interfering in the relationship?

✓ How much uninterrupted face-to-face time do the partners have on a daily basis? Do they feel this is adequate or would they like to change it?

✓ You may want to bundle this practice with Tool #20, *Self-Soothing and Synchronized Breathing*, Tool #25, *Using Affirmations as a Relationship GPS*, and Tool #28, *The Tenderness of Touch and Intimacy*.

Rituals for Coming and Going

If you have ever shaken someone's hand, said goodnight to your partner, used the words "excuse me," when bumping into someone, or recited grace before a meal, you have used a ritual.

There are so many rituals in everyday life that we often don't even think about them. Rituals ease our communications with others. More than that, they bring a sense of normality into the day. They give us the sense that all is right with the world. In our relationships, rituals take on yet another important role. They help us to feel safe, connected, and included. How you enter and leave a space—and how you respond during those times with your partner or friends—can either strengthen or weaken relationships. Use the reflections below to create rituals that promote positive feelings and closeness.

You can use the following reflections for any kind of relationship. Ideally, partners will fill out these reflections on their own and then compare notes.

PART 1 — *Rituals for Leaving—Encouraging Feelings of Closure and Connection*

Reflections

When you physically leave your home (or other space), what behaviors or actions or words do you use with others? For example, do you say "goodbye," shake hands, give a hug or a kiss?

_____

_____

_____

_____

Do you have a sense of closure with your leaving or goodbye ritual? How does it feel for you?

_____

_____

_____

_____

Does your goodbye ritual include a message of how you will stay connected later? What would a connection ritual look or sound like?

_____

_____

_____

_____

When you stay home and your partner or other family members leave, how do you provide a sense of connection for them?

_____

_____

_____

_____

If there was one little thing your partner could do for you in the morning when you are leaving the house that would give you a sense of secure and safe transition, what would that be? (Such as getting out of bed and giving you a kiss, wishing you a good day, etc.)

_____

_____

_____

_____

If there was one little thing your partner could do for you in the evening before going to bed (sleep is another kind of "leaving") what would that look or sound like?

_____

_____

_____

_____

PART 2 — *Rituals for Entering—Encouraging Feelings of Safety and Inclusion*

Reflections

When you physically enter your home (or other space), what behaviors or actions or words do you use with others? For example, do you say "hello," shake hands, give a hug or a kiss? If you skip this ritual step, what do you do? If you bring your stresses of the workday home with you, how does that affect your ability to smoothly reconnect with others in a safe way?

_____

_____

_____

_____

How well does your entering ritual offer you and others a sense of safety and inclusion? How does it feel?

_____

_____

_____

_____

Does your entering ritual include physical contact and eye contact? If not, what might an entering ritual look or sound like?

_____

_____

_____

When you return home, how are you greeted and welcomed by your partner (or others)? How does this make you feel safe and included?

_____

_____

_____

If there was one little thing your partner could do for you when you return home that would help you feel safe and included, what would that be? (Such as turning off the computer or TV, and coming up to give you hug and a kiss.)

_____

_____

_____

How does it feel in other areas of your life (workplace, friends, etc.) when you "enter"? If you are not getting a warm, safe, included welcome, how can you change that? Could you find one person who could provide that for you?

_____

_____

_____

Conclusions

Congratulations on exploring these small, but important ways of connecting and building relationships when coming or going. Like any skill, implementing these rituals requires patience and practice. Keep using them and see how they work.

Tool #30	# Imagine Your Joyful Next Chapter

Mindful Learning Styles

The following learning styles are compatible with this practice:

Verbal-Linguistic   Social-Interpersonal

Visual-Spatial   Reflective-Intrapersonal

Sound-Musical   Existential-Meaning

Bodily-Kinesthetic-Tactile

THOUGHTS FOR THERAPISTS

It might be a sobering realization, but where we place our attention and the thoughts we have play a role in shaping the physical neural architecture of the brain. That's a hopeful realization too, because it means that no matter how stuck anyone might be, they can use attention to rewire the brain, which in turn will change how one thinks in the future! Sports professionals and others also use focused attention to gain mastery over a wide variety of skills. This is known as *self-directed neuroplasticity*, a term coined by psychiatrist Jeffrey Schwartz, who developed a mindfulness method for focusing away from obsessive-compulsive symptoms.

Research has shown that focusing on future goals can have health benefits. A study with over 80 participants found that those assigned to write about "one's best possible self" and future goals over a period of four days—as compared to a traumatic life event or a random event—displayed a significant increase in subjective well-being and were less upset than those focusing on the traumatic event.[30]

The practice that follows uses visualization and only takes a few minutes. Most importantly, it can offer hope and a picture of the future for those who may have had a difficult divorce or other loss of a relationship.

TIPS FOR WORKING WITH CLIENTS

Even though the following practice has one think about the future, it is a mindfulness practice because it first gets people to embrace and feel present moment joy. Only after experiencing joy is the imagination engaged. It's important to note that this exercise is not about the outcome, but the *process* of getting creative to imagine your future.

✓ This may be a good practice for:
- Clients who have lost loved ones and are unable to imagine a hopeful future.

---

[30] Laura A. King, The health benefits of writing about life goals, *Personality and Social Psychology Bulletin*, 2001, 27(7): 798–807.

- Individuals who have lost a connection with joy.
- Couples and partners who want to create a shared vision of the future.

✓ Engage the learning style of the clients with this practice—meaning they can visualize or journal, or do both.

✓ This practice can be bundled with Tool #26, *Enhance Relationships with a Positive Shared Memory*, and Tool #27, *Identifying Strengths to Build Closeness* as a way to increase or regain positive energy in a relationship.

Imagine Your Joyful Next Chapter

Here is a simple, three-step visualization practice for focusing on how you might move forward in your life. If you find that you focus on the past, or on trauma that has happened to you, this can be a nice way to rewire your brain and provide hope for the future. If you find yourself asking, "Where will my relationship be three or five years from now?" you can either do this alone or try this practice with another.

However you use this, this practice offers the opportunity to get out of limited ways of how you picture your future. Instead, it lets you use joy as the compass that points the direction forward.

Instructions

Find a quiet place where you can journal or close your eyes to visualize. Use whichever method works best for you.

You will be visualizing or writing for 5–10 minutes, or as long as needed. Follow these three steps.

Step 1 — *Locate and Connect with Joy*

Think of a time you felt joyful or were passionate about something.

Visualize how you looked and felt at that joyful time. Feel the hope and optimism that you felt. What does this feel like in your body? Right now, feel the joy you felt before.

If negative thoughts creep in, notice these with a sense of acceptance but without identifying with them. Then, let yourself return to experiencing the essence of joy.

If you don't remember what it was like to be joyful, simply imagine that you are joyful by picturing yourself doing something you enjoy and love to do.

Step 2 — *Stay with Joy as You Imagine Your Future*

Maintaining that feeling of joy, imagine what your joyful future self might look like in 1, 5, or 10 years. Choose whatever time frame you want. Even six months will work if that's what you choose.

Remember to let go of expectations about which direction your joy might lead you. Rather than thinking "this is how it must be," imagine this is how joy could move your life in an unexpected or new direction. Freely let the present experience of joy carry you on a journey toward future joy. Let joy be the driver of this ride!

In addition to choosing how far in the future you want to imagine, you can also choose the area of your life you would like to focus on. You can choose to visualize, for example, how joy could lead you toward a personal or relationship goal or dream related to career, retirement, or getting a home, etc.

Step 3 — *Visualize and Journal*

For 10 minutes, visualize or write the story of how joy helps you move toward your future.

As you do this, pay attention to the character strengths that your joyful self possesses. What strengths might help you on your journey to your future? If these are not strengths you currently have, notice which strengths you might want to develop that would help you reach your next joyful future chapter.

Each week, re-visualize how joy moves you toward being your next joyful future chapter. Fill in missing steps that help you reach your best potential future.

Remember, your future self is an expression of the joy you feel *now*. Don't get too attached or worried about a future outcome.

Reflections

How did finding your joy help you to think differently about a future that you create?

_____

_____

_____

_____

How did this practice help you connect with or think about your strengths?

_____

_____

_____

_____

How did thinking about your future make you think about the things that can assist you both now and in the future?

_____

_____

_____

_____

If you did this with another, what did you learn from sharing your experiences? How can this help you both as you move into a shared joyful future chapter?

_____

_____

_____

_____

Mindfulness Tools for Relationship with Community, Workplace & World

Tool #31 | Be an Inclusive Benefactor

> ## *Mindful Learning Styles*
>
> The following learning styles are compatible with this practice:
>
> - Verbal-Linguistic
> - Visual-Spatial
> - Sound-Musical
> - Bodily-Kinesthetic-Tactile
>
> - Social-Interpersonal
> - Reflective-Intrapersonal
> - Existential-Meaning

THOUGHTS FOR THERAPISTS

Those who spend their time watching the evening news or playing violent video games might be convinced the world is a selfish and cynical place where self-interest and taking from others is the predominant and best way to live. But in truth, the world is filled with kindness, givers, and benefactors. What is a benefactor? Think for a moment about someone in your life who made you feel good. This is someone who had the best wishes for your well-being. While you might not have agreed with everything that person believed or said, you knew that they cared deeply about you. Everyone has experienced someone like that—be it a kindly neighbor, a family member, a friend, or even a stranger.

Interestingly, research shows there are some surprising benefits to acting as a benefactor for others.[31] As compared to reflecting on receiving, thinking about voluntarily giving or being a benefactor increases positive mood. What is more, those who act as benefactors view themselves as capable and caring participants and contributors in the scheme of life.

As the world grows smaller, we have begun to understand how we are interconnected. In traditional mindfulness, one key aspect of any mindfulness practice is being aware of the consequences of one's actions. In other words, how can we act wisely and thoughtfully without producing harm? This is easier said than done. But, of course, that's why it's a "practice." Adopting the mindset of a benefactor is to take a step in the direction of being inclusive with our generosity in a way that goes beyond one's close circle of friends, family, and associates.

TIPS FOR WORKING WITH CLIENTS

The handout provided is a guided meditation that can be visualized or written down. This can be done in a session or as a homework assignment.

---

31 Adam Grant and Jane Dutton, Beneficiary or benefactor, *Psychological Science*, Aug 6, 2012; 23(9): 1033–1039.

✓ The following tools could be used as follow-up practices for expanding awareness of, and a stronger connection with, the larger community that takes so many shapes.

- Tool #16, *Open the Compassionate Heart*, which teaches the Loving-Kindness Mediation.

- Tool #34, *Spread One Kindness Today*.

Be an Inclusive Benefactor

Was there ever someone in your life who helped you out, even in a small way that made you feel good? Or made you feel understood? Whether it was a kind teacher, a friendly neighbor, a family member or friend, that person was a benefactor for you. Typically, it feels good to be near one of these benefactors because they have your best interests at heart. You may not agree with everything they say, but you know they care and are watching out for you in their own way.

For this practice, you will visualize how you've acted as a benefactor in your life. It's important to remember that each of us has an impact in the world. Sometimes, even a small act of generosity and sharing can change the direction of someone's life. Keep in mind that this is not meant as an ego-boosting practice. It is a way of accurately recognizing, honoring, and appreciating how you participate in life and have contributed to the world around you.

Instructions

Find a quiet place where you can sit without interruption. Depending on which you like best, you can either visualize or write down your experience as a benefactor.

For the next 5–10 minutes, write about a recent experience in which you acted as a benefactor for another. This might have been at work or in your relationship. When doing this practice with another, each individual can focus on something that allowed the other person to feel grateful or flourish in some way.

To get the most benefit of this practice, write down or visualize your experience using all your senses as you recall it. Include all the details you can.

As you do this, remember to check in with your body to see how recalling your experience as a benefactor makes you feel.

Reflections

How did it feel in the body as you recalled your experience of helping your partner, or another, to flourish? What new insights did you gain from this experience?

_____

_____

_____

_____

What would it be like to expand your benefactor practice into other areas—such as at work, home, and in the community?

_____

_____

_____

_____

What strengths did you tap into as you recalled being a benefactor? How else might these strengths be used to offer help to an even larger and more inclusive group of persons or community?

_____

_____

_____

_____

If you did this benefactor experience with another, what did you learn from sharing your experiences? How might you work together as benefactors? What would that look and feel like?

_____

_____

_____

_____

Tool #32 | Servant Leadership

Mindful Learning Styles

The following learning styles are compatible with this practice:

Verbal-Linguistic   Reflective-Intrapersonal

Mathematical-Science-Logical   Existential-Meaning

Social-Interpersonal

THOUGHTS FOR THERAPISTS

Given the qualities that mindfulness encourages, it seems ideal for supporting what is known as *servant leadership*. Servant leadership is based on the idea of shared empowerment—helping others to reach their best potential. This is a leadership style oriented toward being a benefactor (see Tool #31, *Be an Inclusive Benefactor*), and prizes the leader's humility and authenticity as opposed to exalting and idealizing the leader.

According to research, mindfulness has been shown to help leaders reduce problems such as burnout, anxiety, and depression. But what effect does mindfulness have on actual leadership behaviors? Does it help leaders put others first? Does it promote a non-centered motivation to lead for the greater good? One study examined over 80 leaders (and the "followers" who worked for them) in various industries, finding that "leader mindfulness was positively associated with follower ratings of humility," as well as associated with the servant leadership characteristics of standing back and authenticity.[32] This hopeful research affirms the importance of a new leadership paradigm that shifts into the "We-Thou" perspective. A servant leadership type of relationship is based on input from each person and is not self-serving.

With the many destructive forces that loom over the modern world, wise and servant leadership is needed more than ever. History, however, reads like a book chronicling the abuse of power, and we all know what destructive power can do. Power abuse goes beyond the world stage and is just as harmful in everyday life—in families, relationships, and workplaces. And so, we must ask: Is it possible to lead without being driven by ego needs, bringing into the equation a true sense of humility and the desire to serve? How can a *constructive, collaborative, and cooperative power* be used in relationships where leadership is required?

Fortunately, mindfulness encourages the act of looking and reflecting inwardly. In this way, we can explore our own motives in a relationship, as well as establish a practice of ethics, humility, and wise leadership.

---

[32] Armin Pircher Verdorfer, Examining mindfulness and its relations to humility, motivation to lead, and actual servant leadership behaviors, *Mindfulness*, April, 2016, DOI: 10.1007/s12671-016-0534-8.

143

TIPS FOR WORKING WITH CLIENTS

If there was abuse of power in a client's family, this is an ideal topic to explore. Someone from this background might, for example, either identify with the power of the abuser or reject that way of behaving—even giving up one's own constructive personal power.

✓ This handout is a reflection that can be done during a session. It can also be done at home and processed at a future time.

✓ Since understanding how the strengths of each partner might be complementary and used collaboratively, consider using this handout with Tool #27, *Identifying Strengths to Build Closeness*, and Tool #39, *The Joy of Presence*.

Servant Leadership

What do you feel about the word "leadership"? Does it make you cringe because you have seen the abuses of leaders—in families, politics, religion, relationships, and so on? Mindfulness training instills and encourages a different kind of leadership—one more based on humility and cooperation. This leadership recognizes that true happiness comes from being of service and enhancing the well-being of others.

Instructions

This exercise is a reflection, where you reflect inwardly to explore your views on exercising leadership in your relationship. You don't have to get all of the answers today. After all, empowering co-leadership is a process that you and your partner, or others you work with, will continue to grow and refine.

Partners will separately complete these reflections and then share notes afterwards.

Reflections

In your family history, what did leadership or power look like? Was it used in a fair or unfair way, and how has this shaped your own relationship to leadership?

_____

_____

_____

_____

Do you actively seek or avoid a leadership role in different areas of your life? What do you either worry most about, or enjoy most about having a leadership role in your relationship or other life area?

_____

_____

_____

_____

There is a kind of leadership called "servant leadership" that is based on empowering others to reach their best potential for the benefit of the relationship or work group. This type of leadership recognizes humility, as well as standing back and letting others do their job. If you adopted this style of leadership, how would that change your relationship with your partner (or others)?

_____

_____

_____

_____

Can you think of a specific example of how you would benefit from having your partner stand back and let you take on certain responsibilities? What would be the most difficult thing about this? What would be the easiest thing?

_____

_____

_____

_____

On the flip side, can you think of a specific example of how you might benefit from standing back so your partner could take on certain jobs or roles? What would be the most difficult thing about this? What would be the easiest thing?

_____

_____

_____

_____

On a separate piece of paper, draw a visual map of what leadership looks like in your relationship. You can draw this any way you like to depict what power or leadership in the relationship feels like for you. How are things unilateral or cooperative? What would make the map fit more into the servant leadership model of empowerment and collaboration?

_____

_____

_____

_____

Physically, how does your body move when it uses power or leadership in a non-servant leadership way? Stand and move to see how that feels.

_____

_____

_____

_____

Now, see how your body responds through posture and movement when you assume a more humble, giving, empowering way of working with another.

_____

_____

_____

_____

Follow-Up

Share your findings with your partner (or others) as you go through your reflections. You can re-create and compare your body movement and postures as well.

Afterwards, explore how to create empowering and collaborative leadership in your relationship. Look over the five steps of empowerment below, as found in leadership expert John Baldoni's *Great Motivation Secrets of Great Leaders*.[33] Although originally described for business leaders, I have added in a dash of mindfulness and adapted these suggestions for empowering all relationships.

1. *Identify Opportunities* — Leaders find ways of helping others cooperate and collaborate. This is viewing the relationship as a team—*we* as opposed to *I*. Make sure you and your partner both feel the responsibility is doable.

2. *Give Responsibility* — What's important is that both persons are in on the decision. Empowering opportunities are neither unilaterally assigned nor taken on without a cooperative discussion and decision. Anyone has the power to say no, but try to encourage participation, making sure to explain why this is helpful for the partnership.

3. *Distribute Authority* — Whoever has the responsibility to do the job must also have the authority to make it happen. For example, if that means making arrangements for a vacation trip or purchasing a large item, then that person must be trusted to make the final decision. This doesn't mean the other partner can't be available for consultation if needed, but this isn't imposed or expected.

4. *Hold Your Partner Accountable* — If things don't go as expected, a mindful approach applies acceptance and compassion. But at the same time, this is something both partners can learn from. Taking responsibility for the good *and* the bad is part of personal growth, and the growth of the relationship.

5. *Empower Unto Others* — Once empowerment takes hold it tends to spread. For example, how can others in your family take on additional responsibilities and the authority to make decisions? Empowering is liberating because it creates a synergy and team atmosphere that is both energizing and joyful.

---

[33] John Baldoni, *Great Motivation Secrets of Great Leaders* (New York: McGraw-Hill, 2005), pp. 107–109.

Tool #33	# One-Minute Technology and Workplace Vacation

Mindful Learning Styles

This mental rehearsal tool can be used to imagine many ways of getting present:

Visual-Spatial   Social-Interpersonal

Bodily-Kinesthetic-Tactile   Reflective-Intrapersonal

Sound-Musical   Natural World

THOUGHTS FOR THERAPISTS

According to the American Psychological Association's survey of Stress in America™, almost a quarter of those surveyed reported dealing with extreme stress.[34] In addition, about two-thirds of all persons experience a physical or psychological symptom of stress. Many bring those stresses home from the workplace in various ways such as through mistreating or abusing those in their household or eating in a mindless and unhealthy way. Another big life stressor is the technology that is supposed to make life easier. That's because, ironically, people get very stressed when their technology doesn't work as planned![35]

But it's not just the stress one encounters, but *how one perceives that stress* that matters. For example, when someone views stress as a challenge or obstacle that can be problem-solved, that individual has a greater sense of control and mastery. Viewed from this perspective, stress can offer the opportunity to develop better coping skills. In addition, it's important to recognize that most stress is temporary, that it ebbs and flows. All of these are reasons to not take stress as seriously, and to use tools that can help manage it.

It can also help to have clients start rating their stress levels on a 1–10 scale (1=very low stress to 10=extreme stress). This way they can begin to notice if there are patterns to when stress tends to rise and peak. The practice of rating stress will also help individuals gain greater awareness of what stress feels like in the body at its very earliest stages. Clients can then take immediate action to manage stress before the symptoms get too intense, such as before a headache turns into a migraine or before a mild stomach upset becomes debilitating.

Finally, as a helpful tool, you may want to have clients take the Epstein Stress-Management Inventory for Individuals (ESMI-i).[36] The online 28-question inventory takes only 10 minutes to complete. The inventory can be completed in session or at home, and it provides a quick snapshot of one's stress level.

---

[34] "Stress Snapshot," http://www.apa.org/news/press/releases/stress/2015/snapshot.aspx (accessed April 2017).

[35] https://www.apa.org/news/press/releases/stress/2017/technology-social-media.PDF (accessed September 2017).

[36] http://mystressmanagementskills.com (accessed May 2017).

There are many bundled tools mentioned below for working with stress. The ones in this handout are one way to start. Since there is no single way to relax the body and deal with work stress, feel free to adapt this tool as needed.

TIPS FOR WORKING WITH CLIENTS

Mindfulness has been shown to be helpful in dealing with stress.

✓ Consider bundling this practice with the following tools as a way to reduce and manage stress in the workplace, to take a break from technology, or any time you're feeling overwhelmed:

- Tool #20, *Self-Soothing and Synchronized Breathing*, for turning on the body's built-in relaxation and equilibrium system.
- The fundamental Mindfulness Body/Breath/Mind Meditation that uses Tools #12, #13, and #14.
- Tool #21, *The Power of Acceptance and Patience*, can help one assume a helpful attitude for dealing with things that we may not be able to change or control—at least not in the present moment.

✓ Use this handout as a readable script to guide the client through this practice. Then, the client can take the handout to practice at home.

✓ Ideally, this practice will work better the more it is practiced. Consider scheduling practice times with much repetition so that this will be natural and easy to remember when needed.

One-Minute Technology and Workplace Vacation

It only takes a few moments to rejuvenate yourself with a mental vacation. Research shows that mental rehearsal—long used in sports and the military—works because when you vividly picture yourself doing something the brain responds as if you are actually experiencing that event.

So enjoy the one-minute vacation you are about to take. Best of all, these are portable vacations, so you can take them with you wherever you happen to be. Take a mental vacation anytime you feel worn out, uncreative, stressed, or uninspired. These will be helpful because they will also give you a break from technology overload.

Instructions

Find a quiet spot where you can sit undisturbed for a minute or two. You can do this visualization for longer, but 1–2 minutes is effective.

Before starting, spend a few seconds pressing your heels into the floor or press your hands together if you are lying down. This is just to help you get grounded. Next take two or three long, relaxing breaths, exhaling slowly to get more relaxed and release tension.

Now, follow along with the visualization:

- Recall a vacation place where you felt at ease, relaxed, and rejuvenated.
- Close your eyes and vividly picture the place where you took your vacation. See it in as much detail as possible, using all your senses. If it was at the beach, for example, let yourself smell the ocean breeze, hear the ocean surf tumbling onto the shoreline, feel the warmth of the sun on your body and the sand on your feet, and smell the scent of the fresh air or tanning lotion. Feel your body sink deeply into the towel or sand.
- If you are participating in an activity during your visualization, such as swimming, surfing, hiking, skiing, etc., visualize your movements and surroundings.
- Continue your visualization for one to two minutes.
- Notice any changes in your body—breathing, movement, energy, and respiration—that correspond with your visualization. Even as you open your eyes, let yourself continue to bask in the good feelings and rejuvenation that this mental vacation brings. Carry it with you, feeling refreshed as you continue with your day.

Reflections

How did your one-minute vacation feel? Did you notice changes in the body?

_____

_____

_____

_____

Since this practice works best with repetition, how could you best schedule practicing this skill?

_____

_____

_____

_____

What signals—such as headaches, tension, muscle tightness, or other feelings—let you know that it's time to take a one-minute workplace vacation? Consider using the practice before stress gets too intense or extreme.

_____

_____

_____

_____

Tool #34 | Spread One Kindness Today

Mindful Learning Styles

The following learning styles are compatible with this practice:

Visual-Spatial   Social-Interpersonal

Bodily-Kinesthetic-Tactile   Reflective-Intrapersonal

Sound-Musical

THOUGHTS FOR THERAPISTS

Considering how often clients come to seek help because of struggles, disappointments, and loss, it should come as no surprise they may have a dim view of human nature. Fortunately, the antidote to pessimism may be a dose of kindness. The Dalai Lama addressed the importance of kindness when he wrote:

> *The ultimate source of happiness is not money and power,*
> *but warm-heartedness.*[37]

All the wisdom traditions emphasize altruism and helping others. This makes sense because being kind to others or receiving kindness makes us feel good and be happier. But there are other benefits. One research study, for example, showed that a regular kindness practice increased longevity—actually producing a lower mortality rate over a five-year period as compared to persons who did not help others.[38] There is also evidence that giving kindness produces even more kindness. In other words, pro-social behavior stimulates pro-social behavior in others—much like it did in the movie *Pay It Forward*.

In essence, if we are not kind to ourselves, how can we truly offer this gift to others? This is a multi-faceted tool for becoming softer and gentler with our worldly interactions.

TIPS FOR WORKING WITH CLIENTS

✓ This handout and practice can work well with Tool #22, *Get C.U.R.I.O.U.S.*, and Tool #25, *Using Affirmations as a Relationship GPS*.

  • If using Tool #25, think about including an affirmation for kindness.

✓ This tool is best used by tracking and writing down the different kindnesses that were experienced.

---

[37] 100 Dalai Lama Quotes that Will Change Your Life, https://addicted2success.com/quotes/100-dalai-lama-quotes-that-will-change-your-life/ (accessed May 2017).

[38] Stephanie Brown, Dylan Smith, et al., Caregiving behavior is associated with decreased mortality risk, *Psychological Science*, 2009; 20(4): 488–494.

✓ Explore the idea of using a "kindness jar" or "kindness cup" with this practice. That means that each time during the day that you use a kindness, you can put a penny in the cup, along with a little note of what occurred.

- At the end of the week, look back and see how many kindnesses were offered. Simply count the pennies and review the kindnesses.

Spread One Kindness Today

Think for a moment about a kindness that you received in this past week. How did even the smallest kindness—a smile, a word of encouragement, or a helping hand—make you feel? If it made you happy, appreciative, or affirmed, here's your chance to pay kindness forward. Kindness is also an opportunity to get creative in your life. That's because the opportunity to offer kindness comes when you least expect it. How you offer it is unique to you.

Consider, too, that kindness is a builder of hope and happiness. Doing one kind thing lets you participate in the world in a positive and meaningful way. Best of all, it invites more heartfelt smiles into your life.

As you express kindness, know that you are lending hope and happiness to others, one little building block at a time.

Instructions

To prime and ready yourself for kindness, reflect on the following:

Think of a recent kindness *someone did for you*. How did it feel? How did it make you feel about this kind, giving person?

_____

_____

_____

_____

Think of a recent kindness you gave to another. What did this feel like? How do you think it made the other person feel?

_____

_____

_____

_____

There is no small act of kindness. But if you are up for a challenge, consider doing one of the following—at work or home:

- Compliment someone you have a problem with.
- Anonymously buy a cup of coffee for the person waiting in line behind you.
- When you're in a hurry, step aside and let someone get in front of you in line.
- Talk kindly to someone you might otherwise ignore.
- Compromise with, or forgive, someone who you disagree with.

For the next week, continue to consciously do one kind thing each day. Remember to keep a log of these kindnesses.

Follow-Up After a Week

After looking over a week's worth of kindnesses what do you notice? What was surprising or unexpected by doing one kind thing a day?

_____

_____

_____

_____

What was the most challenging aspect of this practice? What was the easiest?

_____

_____

_____

_____

What is one way that a kindness made a difference to someone close to you?

_____

_____

_____

_____

How did this practice make you feel or change your perspective on things? How could it benefit your relationships?

_____

_____

_____

_____

How could you bring a kindness practice into your life on a consistent basis? What might that look like?

_____

_____

_____

_____

Tool #35 | The Gift of Forgiveness

Mindful Learning Styles

The following learning styles are compatible with this practice:

Verbal-Linguistic   Mathematical-Science-Logical

Visual-Spatial   Social-Interpersonal

Sound-Musical   Reflective-Intrapersonal

Bodily-Kinesthetic-Tactile   Existential-Meaning

THOUGHTS FOR THERAPISTS

Could forgiveness really be a gift? I once had the opportunity to interview Eva Kor, who as a young girl was taken prisoner and sent to the Auschwitz concentration camp in Germany during World War II.[39] Eva and her twin sister were taken to a special barracks that housed identical twins. These twins were treated as guinea pigs and experimented on. When one twin died because of an experiment, the other was immediately killed so that double autopsies could determine the differences. As monstrous as this incarceration was, Eva vowed to survive, and amazingly, she did. But she did not escape from being deeply scarred from the wounds of trauma and anger.

It's worth asking the question: *If something like this had happened to any of us, how would we go about forgiving? Would we even consider it?*

It was many years later when Eva realized she still lived in a prison cell—but this time it was of her own making and constructed out of an unquenchable anger toward those who had committed such inhumane acts. It was then, in an effort to get free, that Eva did what some of her fellow concentration camp survivors considered unthinkable: She forgave. Furthermore, she decided to share this gift of forgiveness with others by traveling worldwide and teaching schoolchildren how to heal through the power of forgiving.

Forgiving is a courageous act that drastically changes relationships. It may even seem to transcend logic. But the fact is that forgiveness helps us move beyond negative emotions and restores hope. It changes our relationship to the self and others by no longer being controlled by anger. As the story of Eva Kor's journey points out, forgiveness is a choice. No one but the one who was hurt has the power to forgive. That's what makes forgiveness such a special gift.

Philosopher Joanna North defined forgiveness as, "When unjustly hurt by another, we forgive when we are overcome with resentment toward the offender, not by denying our right to the resentment, but

---

[39] Donald Altman, *The Mindfulness Code* (Novato, CA: New World Library, 2010), pp. 230–234.

157

instead by trying to offer the wrongdoer compassion, benevolence, and love; as we give these, we as forgivers realize that the offender does not necessarily have a right to such gifts."[40]

TIPS FOR WORKING WITH CLIENTS

Forgiveness is a process, often a long and winding one. Consider the handout as a beginning step on a long journey. One place to explore is to look at how forgiveness played a role in one's family. Was forgiveness freely given and viewed as strength? Or was it seen as a sign of weakness?

Also, consider exploring the following ideas when working with forgiveness:

✓ Forgiving doesn't mean that the forgiver has to do anything different or reach out to the offender. The forgiver doesn't even have to say anything to that person.

✓ Read the instructions as a meditation in session, and then use the reflections to explore afterwards.

✓ When working with forgiveness, consider bundling this handout with the following ones for building compassion and acceptance:

  • Tool #15, *Accepting the Unwanted and Rejected*

  • Tool #16, *Open the Compassionate Heart*

  • Tool #21, *The Power of Acceptance and Patience*

[40] Robert Enright, *Forgiveness Is a Choice* (Washington, DC: APA LifeTools, 2001), p. 25.

The Gift of Forgiveness Meditation

If you're reading this, you may have had a relationship issue that caused anger or resentment that is difficult to accept, let alone forgive. The truth is, forgiving can be hard. For those who have been abused or mistreated, it might seem that forgiving is a mistake or a weakness. And then there's the fact that sometimes, holding onto hurts and anger can feel good. It can give someone a sense of control and righteousness. And, it might feel that anger is necessary to prevent further abuse and injustice. Those are all valid points.

Ultimately, if you've been hurt, no one but you can decide whether or not to forgive. And that is exactly what makes forgiveness an extraordinary gift—one given to someone who may not really deserve it. You don't have to do anything different after making this choice, and the one you forgive may not even know—and that's okay.

But in the long term, you have to ask if continuing to feed the flames of anger is helping or hindering your life. If you do decide to forgive, you might do it for the selfish reason that it helps you and gives you hope. It doesn't mean you will forget or let abuse happen again. That's important to know.

With that said, this handout is a meditation and exploration into forgiveness.

Instructions

Find a comfortable and safe place to sit where you won't be interrupted. Close your eyes and take two or three nice comforting breaths.

Remind yourself that you are in a safe place. If at any time during this practice you feel distressed, you can open your eyes and decide to do this practice later.

You will imagine two scenarios. **In the first scenario, you will imagine yourself 10 years in the future still harboring anger and resentment** toward whomever or whatever caused you hurt. **In the second scenario, you will imagine your future self after having forgiven.**

Note: This can be done as a complete mental visualization, or by changing between two chairs—one representing the present self, and the other representing the future self. When seated in the "future self-chair," you can verbally respond to the questions being asked.

Scenario 1 — *Future Self Holding onto Anger, Resentment, Hurt*

Mentally picture the image of yourself 10 years into the future sitting opposite you.

Spend a few moments now to introduce yourself to this future self. Let it know that you have come to explore how the choice not to forgive has worked for you through the years. Let this self know that you feel a strong sense of respect, connection, and compassion for it. You simply want to get more information.

PAUSE after each question to get the answer—either mentally picturing it or by switching to the other chair.

Question and Answer

Q: I'm really curious to know what it has been like for you to hold onto this anger for 10 more years. How has that affected you personally—I mean physically and emotionally or otherwise?

Q: Now that you decided to hold onto that anger, how has that affected your attitude about people and your life in general?

Q: What happened to that relationship that caused you pain since you held onto anger? Even if the relationship ended, or even if that person has passed away, how has holding onto the anger helped you?

Q: Since you've been living like this for 10 years, do you ever think there would be a time that you'd be willing to let go of this anger and forgive, even a little bit? And if you did this how do you think it might affect your next 10 years?

Q: Is there anything else you'd like to share with me? Thank you for spending this time with me. I may want to consult with you in the future if that's okay.

Scenario 2 — *Future Self Letting Go of Anger, Resentment, Hurt*

Q: Thank you for spending this time with me. I'm really curious to know what it has been like for you to have forgiven and let go of anger for these 10 years. How has that affected you personally—I mean physically and emotionally?

Q: When you decided to let go of anger and resentment, what was the hardest thing about doing that? What made you finally decide to take that step to offer that gift?

Q: How did this change affect your ability to experience joy? Did it affect your attitude about people and your life in general? Do you still feel safe? Did you forget? I know that's a lot of questions!

Q: What happened to the relationship that caused you pain since you let go of anger? Even if the relationship ended, or even if that person has passed away, how has letting go of the anger helped you?

Q: Since you've been living like this for 10 years, what's the biggest difference you've noticed in your life? And if I were to start thinking about letting go of my anger, what advice do you have for me?

Q: Is there anything else you'd like to share with me? Thank you for spending this time with me. I may want to consult with you in the future if that's okay.

Reflections

Sit for a few moments longer to reflect on your experiences in exploring forgiveness with your future self. What new thoughts or insights do you have?

_____

_____

_____

_____

| Tool #36 | # Building Trust that Lasts |

Mindful Learning Styles

The following learning styles are compatible with this practice:

Verbal-Linguistic   Social-Interpersonal

Visual-Spatial   Reflective-Intrapersonal

Sound-Musical   Existential-Meaning

Mathematical-Science-Logical

THOUGHTS FOR THERAPISTS

Relationships require strong foundational pillars to make them really enduring and strong. Without possessing what I called the "Three Seeds of Relationship" in my book *Clearing Emotional Clutter*, a loving, mutual, and caring relationship would not survive.[41] The three seeds, or pillars, are trust, empathy, and acceptance. If any of these gets weak or erodes, then the relationship will struggle.

Earlier in *The Mindfulness Toolbox for Relationships*, various tools explored how mindfulness is compatible with building acceptance and empathy. Similarly, mindfulness plays a role in trust. As an example of this, a study in the *Journal of Loss and Trauma* looked at over 500 college students who had experienced trauma. They found that at lower levels of PTSD, mindfulness was associated with greater trust.[42] Once trust is firmly cemented in place, relationships of all kinds can get through stormy weather.

While broken trust can be rebuilt over time—and I've worked with clients who needed to do that—it's easier to maintain trust by using the handout and practice that follows.

TIPS FOR WORKING WITH CLIENTS

✓ This practice can be done individually or with another.

- Each person has a handout and then explore their answers together.

✓ Try bundling this practice with the following:

- Tool #16, *Open the Compassionate Heart*
- Tool #20, *Self-Soothing and Synchronized Breathing*
- Tool #23, *Grow Your Compassion Container*
- Tool #27, *Identifying Strengths to Build Closeness*

---

41   Donald Altman, *Clearing Emotional Clutter* (Novato, CA: New World Library, 2016), pp. 92–95.

42   Megan Kuhl and Güler Boyraz, Mindfulness, general trust, and social support among trauma-exposed college students, *Journal of Loss and Trauma,* 2017; 22(2).

Building Trust that Lasts

No relationship instantly begins with a deep well of trust. Long-lived trust builds mutually and slowly, little by little through shared cooperation, respect, and taking an interest in what another has to offer. Trust builds bridges of safety to others. The following practice helps build and maintain those bridges.

Instructions

The next time you are with someone, try building trust through the steps on the following checklist. You can even think about a recent relationship interaction and review it on the basis of this trust-building checklist.

- **Listen to Your Gut**
  - Are there any red flags or doubts you feel or sense?
  - If there are any signals making you unsure if you are safe, slow down. You can always get those doubts or questions answered at a later time.
  - Remember that **trust takes time.** So don't rush it.

- **Mutual Attentiveness and Listening**
  - Because mutuality builds trust, you can do your part by making sure the interaction is not one-sided. That means allowing the other to share as you listen with undivided attention.
  - Let go of your own agenda—at least for the moment.
  - See if you can be free of judgment and personal bias.

- **Take an Open Body Posture**
  - A non-defensive body posture and open gestures—such as not crossing the arms over the chest—are important for trust building. Make appropriate eye contact.

- **Be Curious**
  - Let yourself get curious, like a detective who wants to know more. Letting someone be at ease is a good way to understand that person. Through understanding another, you can know if you feel safe.
  - Take an active interest in the ideas, hobbies, and life of the one you are with. Whether you've known this person for a short or long time, continuing to take an interest lets them know you care.

- **Be Honest While Empathizing**
  - As the old saying goes, "put yourself in the other person's shoes." You might not agree, and you can share your perspective while being respectful. At least you can try to see what things look like from their perspective. Remember, too, that honesty also means following through on your word and being dependable. Without honoring your word, trust cannot grow.

- **Accept the Imperfections**
  - Who's perfect? If you really want to build trust, try accepting those things you *don't* like about someone. This doesn't mean accepting things that are unkind, harmful, or abusive. But it means that you know that person is a human with frailties. When you can accept another's frailties, they can accept yours. This is an important test and building block of trust.

Reflections

Which of the above trust-building items, if any, was new to you? How have you used these items in the past to build trust?

_____

_____

_____

_____

Which of these practices is the easiest? Which do you find most challenging?

_____

_____

_____

_____

Because trust building is mutual, how do close persons in your life use these practices? How does that affect your relationships and make you feel?

_____

_____

_____

_____

What is one positive change that might come from using the practices above?

_____

_____

_____

_____

Tool #37 | Softening with G.L.A.D.

THOUGHTS FOR THERAPISTS

Gratitude is a coping skill that not only gets someone out of the head, but infuses life with new meaning. Research shows that the practice of gratitude reduces symptoms of depression and builds resilience. It's also worth noting that the feeling of gratitude is incompatible with some negative feeling states such as envy and jealousy. When you think about it, gratitude is really a mindfulness practice because it teaches how to use one's attention. For example, one can focus on the things that are missing from life, or one can choose to focus on the good, the decent, and the beautiful things that life has to offer. This is not to say that life doesn't have challenges, but that life offers a rich and diverse menu of items. Sometimes, we need to turn toward those things that are inspiring, uplifting, and pleasing.

In workshops, I often mention four different kinds of gratitude. There is basic gratitude that we could have for the necessities of life, such as warmth from the sun, running water, clothes to keep us warm, and so on. These might seem commonplace, but without these basics, life would be filled with suffering, if not impossible. Secondly there is personal gratitude, which includes things that personally support us, such as a job, our health, having transportation, and more. Thirdly, there is relationship gratitude. These are the many relationships that nourish and enrich our lives. Lastly is paradoxical gratitude. This is having gratitude for the things you wish you *didn't* have in your life! You might also think of this as "silver lining" gratitude—finding the lesson or silver lining within that difficult life challenge or obstacle.

I developed this G.L.A.D. practice some years back as a way to help people get into the here and now moment and find positives that go beyond just finding gratitude. The practice here helps soften skepticism and cynicism, and the hardening of the heart that happens all too frequently in today's world.

Many clinicians who have used G.L.A.D. have shared with me many different, wonderful ways of applying it. In these pages, it's going to be used as a relationship practice.

TIPS FOR WORKING WITH CLIENTS

It can help to introduce clients to gratitude to see how well they accept the idea of using it. Sharing research can be helpful to get buy-in. What makes the G.L.A.D. practice different is that it offers a broad range of methods for noticing the outside world and softening the heart with new hope.

✓ Optionally, clients can use the G.L.A.D. practice with another person. Each can share his or her emotions before and after the practice.

✓ The following practices fit nicely for bundling with the G.L.A.D. handout:

- Tool #16, *Open the Compassionate Heart*
- Tool #24, *S.T.O.P. the Relationship Robot of Reactivity*
- Tool #26, *Enhance Relationships with a Positive Shared Memory*

Softening with G.L.A.D.

There are a lot of things in life that can harden our view, making us more rigid in our views, as well as more fearful, guarded, skeptical, and cynical. In fact, this is what happens when you encounter stress over and over. It becomes easier to erect a protective wall. The problem is that wall keeps out the good things, too!

Here is a practice that can soften your view by letting you notice the good, decent, and beautiful things that life has to offer. Yes, life has those things that may be causing you stress, but it also has the good things.

Attention is selective, and where you focus your attention determines your memories and experience. This simple four-part acronym can help keep things in balance and give you a fresh perspective.

Instructions

Each day, individuals, partners, friends, families, or other groups that are using this practice can share their experiences at some point, such as at the end of the day or at dinnertime. Throughout the day, take a mental snapshot or write down each of the following items.

If you want to focus on relationship gratitude, do the practices in boldface.

G — *One Gratitude*

- Find one thing you were grateful for or appreciated this week.
- **One thing about your partner (friend, etc.) that you're grateful for.**

L — *One Learning*

- Something new you learned today.
- **One new thing you learned about your partner (friend, etc.) today.**

A — *One Accomplishment*

- One act of self-care, such as getting enough sleep and nourishment.
- **One accomplishment made by your partner (friend, etc.) today.**

D — *One Delight*

- Anything that makes you feel joyful or happy, such as hearing a bird chirp, seeing a flower, laughing at a joke, tasting food, returning a smile, noticing a pleasant sensation, etc.
- **One delightful experience related to your relationship.**

Reflections

What was it like to notice the four elements of the G.L.A.D. practice? Which of these was the easiest for you? Which was the most challenging?

_____

_____

_____

_____

If you did this alone, what did you notice? How did this change how you experienced the day? Did this practice soften you in some way?

_____

_____

_____

_____

If you did this practice with another, what was it like to share your experiences? What was it like when you heard the other person's experiences?

_____

_____

_____

_____

The G.L.A.D. method is like any skill that needs practice and repetition. How could this practice be integrated into your life as a daily or weekly practice? What would this look like? What changes would you need to make?

_____

_____

_____

_____

This practice can also be used to counter stress in the moment. How could G.L.A.D. be adapted as a stress management tool?

_____

_____

_____

_____

Tool #38	# H.E.A.L. with Cooperative Listening

Mindful Learning Styles

The following learning styles are compatible with this practice:

Verbal-Linguistic   Mathematical-Science-Logical

Visual-Spatial   Social-Interpersonal

Sound-Musical   Reflective-Intrapersonal

Bodily-Kinesthetic-Tactile   Existential-Meaning

THOUGHTS FOR THERAPISTS

David Bohm was more than one of the world's leading quantum physicists. Bohm also worked to develop methods that promoted open and cooperative communication. In his book *On Dialogue* he acknowledged the difficulties inherent in accomplishing this, writing, "For one thing, everybody has different assumptions and opinions. They are basic assumptions—not merely superficial assumptions—such as assumptions about the meaning of life; about your own self-interest, your country's interest, or your religious interest; about what you really think is important. And these assumptions are defended when they are challenged."[43] If two people in a relationship cannot get along or listen without defensiveness, how can the world ever hope to attain even a small measure of peace?

Since mindfulness teaches how to observe and be less attached to our basic assumptions, it holds the potential to transform relationships. Tool #36, *Building Trust that Lasts*, touched upon some of the aspects of cooperative listening that will be brought into greater focus here. To support mutually satisfying relationships, the acronym H.E.A.L. can help anyone listen with greater openness and love.

TIPS FOR WORKING WITH CLIENTS

✓ This practice is a useful skill to work on for clients who get easily triggered or defensive when in conversations.

✓ Partners and others can both learn this practice and go through the steps and the reflections together.

✓ This tool matches up well with Tool #36, *Building Trust that Lasts*. Consider pairing up these two practices.

    • Tool #20, *Self-Soothing and Synchronized Breathing*, can be used before a difficult conversation, as a means of bringing partners into a calm alignment.

---

[43] David Bohm, *On Dialogue* (London: Routledge Classics, 1996/2004), pp. 8–9.

H.E.A.L. with Cooperative Listening

Do you ever get defensive when talking with a significant person in your life? That happens to everyone. And when that happens, the stress response makes it difficult for us to listen. Worse, discordant events like this, if habitual, can cause harm and damage to a relationship. Fortunately, the following practice offers a way to cool yourself down, even as you are listening to another.

Instructions

The acronym that follows can give you greater skill at listening to another in a way that lowers reactivity and defensiveness. Write this acronym down on a note card and practice the steps so that you remember them.

This practice doesn't mean you can't have an opinion, but that you can listen in a new way. You might find that you can strengthen relationships with this method.

Use this practice in the moment—anytime you notice that things are heating up and that you're feeling defensive.

H — *Hold Assumptions*

No matter what you might believe, it's not possible to make space for another's ideas and thoughts if your "cup" is filled to the brim with your own preconceived ideas and biases. Empty your cup of your own assumptions even for five minutes. Then get curious about where the other person is coming from.

E — *Empathy to Engage, Not Enrage*

Step into the emotional world of the person with whom you are conversing. Do this by having empathy for their plight and feelings. Can you feel their feelings? Empathy engages others, whereas being closed or defensive can enrage.

A — *Absorb and Accept*

Be like a sponge that takes in all you hear. Absorbing another's perspective can take time, so absorb as much as you can. Acceptance doesn't mean you agree, but that you can accept this is where things are right now. Acceptance means you don't need to try to fix anything. Just take it in and accept the moment.

L — *Lead with Respect and Kindness*

So after you've done all of the above, what happens next? How do you reply or respond? Whatever you do, lead with respect and kindness. If you are not able to do that in the moment—and that's okay—let this person know that you would like time to think about what has been said. Sometimes, we need to reflect before we can respect. You can step back and tap your wisdom and insight, or consult with a wise friend or mentor. If you cannot speak without anger, wait until you are ready to respond with respect, kindness, and compassion.

Reflections

What was it like to use the H.E.A.L. practice? Which of these steps was the easiest for you? Which was the most challenging?

_____

_____

_____

_____

When is a time you can you use the H.E.A.L. practice? Who might you want to use this with?

_____

_____

_____

_____

What is one positive thing that could come from using this practice during an argument or disagreement?

_____

_____

_____

_____

How might this affect a relationship or make talking about a difficult topic a little easier? How useful would it be for a partner to also use this practice?

_____

_____

_____

_____

How could you practice this so that you could easily remember it—even in the heat of the moment? What would that practice look like?

_____

_____

_____

_____

Tool #39 | The Joy of Presence

Mindful Learning Styles

Because this practice is about getting present, anyone can adapt it for his or her mindful learning style:

Verbal-Linguistic   Social-Interpersonal

Visual-Spatial   Reflective-Intrapersonal

Sound-Musical   Natural World

Bodily-Kinesthetic-Tactile   Existential-Meaning

Mathematical-Science-Logical

THOUGHTS FOR THERAPISTS

How often does your mind wander? And when it does, are you feeling happy or unhappy? An ingenious study sought to answer these questions by using a mobile phone app to randomly contact several thousand people.[44] Subjects were asked to identify an activity that they were engaged in right at that moment (e.g. shopping, eating, watching TV, etc.). Then, to determine mind wandering, subjects were asked if they were thinking about that activity or whether they were thinking about something else. Finally, subjects were asked how happy they felt in that moment. The results showed that on average, individuals had wandering minds 46.9% of the time.

Most interestingly, the study found an inverse relationship between mind wandering and self-reports of happiness. This meant that when people's minds wandered the most they were least happy in those moments. However, when people's minds wandered the least they reported themselves as being most happy. Low mind wandering is what scientists call "presence of mind." Researchers found that subjects experienced the most presence (low mind wandering) and highest levels of happiness when fully inhabiting the body—such as when making love, exercising, and engaging in conversation with another person.

According to one of the researchers, Matthew Killingsworth, "mind-wandering appears ubiquitous across all activities. This study shows that our mental lives are pervaded, to a remarkable degree, by the non-present. Mind-wandering is an excellent predictor of people's happiness."[45]

---

44 M. Killingsworth and D. Gilbert, A wandering mind is an unhappy mind, *Science*, 2010, November; 330(6006), 932.

45 "Wandering mind not a happy mind," http://news.harvard.edu/gazette/story/2010/11/wandering-mind-not-a-happy-mind/ (accessed May 2017).

When you bring mindfulness into your relationships, it doesn't matter so much what you're doing but *how present you are* that makes all the difference. Best of all, the quality of your attention enhances mutuality when you are with a partner, child, friend, or colleague—and may very well be the key to happiness.

TIPS FOR WORKING WITH CLIENTS

If a client is especially distracted and reports having a busy mind, this tool will be a helpful one. Distraction and mind wandering can be worked with using the foundational Mindfulness Body/Breath/ Mind Meditation that uses Tools #12, #13, and #14.

✓ Tapping into the client's mindful learning style will help you understand how they get most present. So will activities that tend to ground one in the body. With that in mind, consider bundling this tool with the following:
- Tool #11, *Optimize Communication with Your Mindful Learning Styles*
- Tool #28, *The Tenderness of Touch and Intimacy*

Five Steps to Presence

Did you ever have the experience of being with someone, but they really weren't with you? Maybe they were distracted, looking at their phone or the computer, or maybe they had something else on their mind. We've all experienced this in one form or another. But if it's an ongoing pattern, it doesn't build a sense of mutuality and togetherness.

It's kind of like the little phrase on the back of a carnival or game ticket that reads: "You must be present to win." In the same way, you must give your full presence to the significant persons in your life to have a sustainable relationship that feels joyful and alive.

These five simple steps can bring greater presence and mutuality into any relationship. If you are doing this with a partner, share how it feels to connect in this way.

Instructions

Step 1 — *Get Grounded*

In order to get present with another, you first need to get present with your own self. How do you best get grounded in the here and now? Do you take a breath? Do you rub your hands together? Do you press your feet into the ground? Do you look at nature? Do you think about a favorite quotation? Use your mindful learning style to get present. If you don't know your learning style, see Tip #3, *Identifying and Implementing Mindful Learning Styles*.

Step 2 — *Attune with Self*

If you're going to connect with another, what are you "bringing to the table" in terms of your own emotions and bodily felt sense? If you are tense, it will help you to know that so you can either share that feeling or try to release it. The body holds emotions, and others will sense this. So first, get present and attune with your own felt sense.

By noting and naming the sensations, feelings, and emotions, you will help yourself regulate and get centered. (Tool #14, *Mind Regulation for Making Peace with the Mind*, can be a helpful practice.)

Step 3 — *Attune with Other*

Once you've come into a sense of awareness and attunement with yourself, let yourself attune with your partner or whoever you are with right now. Attuning means noticing how the other is holding the body as well as facial expressions. Use your empathy ability to feel the other person's emotional state. You don't have to say anything about it—unless you sense very obvious emotions such as anger, frustration, or grief. It's enough to let yourself sense and attune. If another is more animated, you might feel yourself getting more animated. If this person's emotions have them being quieter and subdued, then you can attune with that.

Step 4 — *Narrow Focus and Attend*

Shut down the electronics, the phone, and any other distractions that may be grabbing your attention. Bring your focus to the one who is with you right now, right here. Attend to what is happening between you, even being aware of subtle movements and gestures. As well, attend to the needs of the other person and the relationship. If your partner needs comforting, assurance, or laughter, you can attend to that and be supportive in those ways.

Step 5 — *Lean into Presence*

Let your presence be warm, inviting, and welcoming. Be open to the shared experience of now! Leaning into presence means you are not a bystander in the relationship, but are fully participating and engaging in it. Let your presence be felt.

Follow-Up

Take your time in getting familiar with these five steps of "presencing" with others. Practice these steps throughout the day until you eventually bring them all together. You may also want to journal your experiences on how differently interactions feel when using your full presence. See for yourself if greater joy and togetherness result when you use this practice.

Tool #40	# Spontaneous Play

Mindful Learning Styles

The following learning styles are compatible with this practice:

Verbal-Linguistic   Social-Interpersonal

Visual-Spatial   Reflective-Intrapersonal

Sound-Musical   Natural World

Bodily-Kinesthetic-Tactile

THOUGHTS FOR THERAPISTS

There's the word *déjà vu,* which can be defined as "having been there before." The wonderful thing about mindfulness is that it takes us out of rote thinking and behavior, which is why I often describe it as the opposite of déjà vu—or *vujà dé, never having been there before.* This childlike ability to see things for the first time can also mean experiencing those in our life as if for the first time. It means that we can play and rejoice in a spontaneous and mutual way. Play links us firmly to others, a message affirmed by social psychologist Kenneth Gergen when he wrote, "I am linked, therefore I am."[46] I would like to rephrase as, "We are co-linked, therefore we are."

From our experiences on childhood playgrounds to grown-up team sports, play fosters mutuality and teamwork. Dance movement therapist and teacher Maria Brignola wrote, "Mutuality is a creative process in which openness to change allows something new to happen, building on the different contributions of each person. It is not sameness or equality but a way of relating, sharing activity in which each or all persons involved are participating as fully as possible."[47]

For these reasons, play holds the key to taking relationships to a whole new, shared and creative place that might not otherwise be possible. Getting into a mindset of playing might help any relationship get unstuck from old patterns, even in a small way.

TIPS FOR WORKING WITH CLIENTS

It can help to understand how play was expressed in a client's family. Was play common? Was it a reward for work? Was it competitive or cooperative? What is one's attitude toward being spontaneous?

✓ Competitive play, where there is an identified "winner" or "loser," can create ill feelings. How attached is a client to winning?

---

[46] Kenneth Gergen, *Relational Being* (New York: Oxford University Press, 2009), p. 400.
[47] Maria Brignola, *Dance of Relationship Training* (Portland, OR: Marylhurst University, 2017).

- Encourage cooperative play, which has no purpose other than to be fun, spontaneous, and creative.

✓ As warm-ups for this practice, consider bundling with the following four tools:

- Tool #20, *Self-Soothing and Synchronized Breathing*, which involves mirroring and connecting.
- Tool #28, *The Tenderness of Touch and Intimacy*, which includes a mirroring practice.
- Tool #34, *Spread One Kindness Today*, which involves the practice of spontaneous kindness.
- Tool #39, *The Joy of Presence*, which sensitizes one to being attuned and open to the needs of another.

Spontaneous Play

Right now, think back on a time when you enjoyed playing with another. Did you feel connected to others? What made it so thrilling and so much fun? The freedom, lightness, and joy that come from spontaneous play is not just for children. It can be one of the perks of a playful state of mind.

What makes this spontaneous play different from other games you might have played is that there is no defined "winner" or "loser" here. The goal is simply to have fun and be spontaneous and in the moment. In spontaneous play everyone is a "winner" through mutual enjoyment. So what's "the game"?

The game is that there is no game.

Your role is to be spontaneous and in the moment, as if you were part of an improvisational troupe of actors. After all, isn't life really an improvisation? It doesn't matter if you are in the workplace trying to come up with a solution for a problem or at home planning a trip to the grocery store. Each moment presents you with entirely new situations, changing scenarios, and different persons to work with. So here are a few steps to engage in spontaneous play each day to enliven your relationships and get unstuck from your own stale patterns.

Instructions

Identify Your Role(s)

Do you tend to take on a particular role? Often, we assume a role in our family or the workplace—even without trying. A role may feel comfortable because we've been playing that part. What role or roles do you typically assume? Remember, a role in this context is neither good nor bad.

Actors are not permanently the character they are playing, and neither are you the role you take on! Just because you may identify with a role doesn't mean you can't experiment with others—even for a short while. Circle the roles you play.

creative initiator	quiet caretaker of others
loyal follower	detached evaluator
confident know-it-all	needy approval seeker
skeptical resistor	supportive angel
disappearing wallflower	stable provider
harmonizing peacemaker	unpredictable trickster
boisterous, opinionated leader	carefree rogue

Write in other roles you play: _____

Let Go of Your Role(s)

What would it be like for you to not be so attached to your present role? How is any current role confining you and defining you?

The *real* role you can play is to just be *you*, free of the baggage inherent in any role. This is just awareness itself, unfettered and open to possibility. Should you notice you are playing one of the "assigned" roles, allow yourself to release it and let it go.

In the improvisation that is life, you don't have to be defined by past or present roles.

Participate Fully and Lovingly

Any improvisation demands full presence and participation. If you are distracted or mentally elsewhere, then you are not fully present and committed to what is happening right now. Let yourself be more free and open than a particular role might allow for.

Being more spontaneous and free, however, doesn't mean you have the right to harm or be rude to others. Remember that spontaneous play is a non-competitive sport. You'll know it's working when life is more alive, kind, and fun for all involved.

Share the Stage

Since you are not doing spontaneous play alone, make sure to let your partner or others get creative. Allow yourself the ability to shift gears and go with the flow. What gets created in this spirit of play—even at home or at work—can often lead to some very useful and "out of the box" problem solving.

Release Expectations; Embrace the Process

A lot of unnecessary suffering in life comes from the expectations we have about how things are "supposed to be," including how others are "supposed" to act. But how can you truly experience spontaneous play if you're using a predetermined script of what will happen? It is only by letting go of expectations that our relationships become more open, expressive, collaborative, creative, and ultimately, more loving.

Follow-Up

Now that you're familiar with the steps involved in spontaneous play, use the following questions to help decide how to implement it. For example, is there a particular area of your life (parenting, career, relationship, etc.) where being more free—and less attached to a role—might be helpful?

_____

_____

_____

_____

What feels like the biggest challenge for you to improvise, or spontaneously play with others? What's the easiest thing about it? How and where could you try this out?

_____

_____

_____

_____

What is one good thing that could come out of living in a less scripted way and letting go of expectations?

_____

_____

_____

_____

Mindfulness Tools for Relationship with the Natural World

Tool #41 | Forest Bathing Meditation

Mindful Learning Styles

The following learning styles are compatible with this body meditation practice:

Visual-Spatial   Reflective-Intrapersonal

Sound-Musical   Natural World

Bodily-Kinesthetic-Tactile   Existential-Meaning

Social-Interpersonal

THOUGHTS FOR THERAPISTS

It was in the 1970s that two professors at the University of Michigan started to explore how nature could help students who were mentally fatigued. Psychologists Rachel and Stephen Kaplan began investigating the immersive, engaging quality of nature and how it helped to naturally restore depleted mental concentration and focus. Their work led to a field of study known as Attention Restoration Theory. Research in this field has now demonstrated many health benefits of spending time in nature—from speeding up healing to reducing aggression and mental fatigue.

You might think of nature as vitamin N. In Japan, the practice of "forest bathing," or being among trees, was recommended in a public health program as far back as 1982. A recent study showed how spending time in a forest significantly up-regulated, or increased, the number of natural killer (NK) cells in the body.[48] These cells are an important part of the immune system because they fight certain types of viruses and even tumors. Trees in particular cleanse the air and release substances that are medically helpful.

In particular, nature is a counterbalance to technology. When making a trip to nature, alone or with another, it can be helpful to leave the technology behind—or at least turned off.

TIPS FOR WORKING WITH CLIENTS

Keep in mind that the average adult spends up to six hours a day in front of screens. A Kaiser Family Foundation study reported, "Eight- to eighteen-year-olds spend more time with media than in any other activity besides (maybe) sleeping—an average of more than 7-1/2 hours a day, seven days a week."[49]

---

[48] Q. Li, M. Kobayashi, et al., Effect of phytonicide from trees on human natural killer cell function, *International Journal of Immunopathology and Pharmacology*, 2009 Oct–Dec; 22(4): 951–959.

[49] "Generation M2: Media in the Lives of 8- to 18-Year-Olds," https://kaiserfamilyfoundation.files.wordpress.com/2013/04/8010.pdf (Accessed May 2017).

✓ When considering when to use nature, it can be helpful to first assess the level of technology that one uses.

- Daily technology usage.
- Technology before sleep.
- Usage of video games.
- Usage of social media.

✓ Create breaks from technology using nature and social connection.

✓ Consider bundling this practice with other nature practices, including the belly breathing tool mentioned below:

- Tool #20, *Self-Soothing and Synchronized Breathing*, which teaches diaphragmatic breathing.
- Tool #42, *Letting It Be with Sky Gazing*
- Tool #43, *The All-Purpose Nature Transition*

Forest Bathing Meditation

Some of the most soothing and calming things you can encounter are the most ordinary and natural. The idea of forest bathing—just being with trees—is a public health practice that has been used in Japan for many years.

In fact, research shows that nature can be helpful for reducing stress and mental fatigue. More than that, it gives you a time of quiet and peace away from the hectic, always turned-on high tech world. If you feel burned out, mentally fatigued, and unable to focus and be present with those you care about—a nature break, or vitamin N, might be just what you need. Best of all, it's easy to do.

Note: If you do this with another person, don't talk with one another until after going through the entire practice.

Instructions

This may be the easiest practice in these pages! All you have to do is seek out a natural setting, preferably with trees. The benefits of being around trees have been studied, and it's actually beneficial for the immune system.

Set Aside Time

This may seem like an odd instruction, but setting aside time makes the statement that you are making this a priority and taking it seriously. Allow yourself a minimum of 10 minutes to sit in nature—ideally 10–20 minutes. If you haven't done this before and you feel yourself getting impatient, that's normal. It can take time before the body registers that it's okay to relax.

Ideally, set a timer to ring in the allotted time so you don't have to keep checking the time.

If you only have two or three minutes to spend, start there. It's better to do a little forest bathing than none at all!

Set Your Worries and Troubles Aside

Make a mental note to let go of your worries and thoughts for this time period. You might even imagine putting your "to-do list" or other thoughts in a mental filing cabinet that you can re-open after you have completed forest bathing.

Find a Natural Setting

Any trees or greenery will work. Whether it's the courtyard of a business park, your backyard, some trees along the sidewalk, or a park you enjoy visiting. You can stand or sit or walk.

Belly Breathe

Take nice, slow and long breaths as you inhale the fresh air that is being cleansed by the trees. Let these breaths calm and relax you deeply. Let your body relax more with each breath.

Absorb Yourself in Nature

Cast your gaze out to the trees, the grass, the sky, and any other natural object. Don't just look superficially, but let your gaze penetrate deeply the nature with which you co-exist. Allow the mind to rest as you continue to absorb in nature. Get curious as you watch and observe. There's nothing more to do! Just be 100% devoted to being with nature in this moment. And the next moment. And the next.

Reflections

What was it like to sit in nature in this way? What was most challenging about it for you? What was easiest?

_____

_____

_____

_____

How long did it take until you really slowed down? How did this affect (if it did) the busyness of your mind?

_____

_____

_____

_____

How did you refocus on the nature around you when your mind wandered?

_____

_____

_____

_____

What did you notice about nature that you never knew before? What is one way that this practice could provide a benefit for you and a partner?

_____

_____

_____

_____

How could you bring this practice into your day or life on a more consistent basis? What would this look like?

_____

_____

_____

_____

Tool #42 | Letting It Be with Sky Gazing

THOUGHTS FOR THERAPISTS

There are many different ways to reset or regain one's equilibrium after a major life transition, such as going through a divorce or other loss. While cognitive behavioral approaches can help, there are insights and epiphanies that come from touching nature's grace and mystery. This was the case with Rick, a client who had lost hope for his future. His business was struggling—and he knew it was only a matter of time before he might be unemployed. Added to that, Rick's adult son had recently moved back home after a divorce. A menacing, dark storm had appeared over the sunny financial horizon he and his wife had planned and worked for. As he described it to me, each day he would go into his office, unable to focus or work.

Nothing really seemed to help until I told Rick about the sky gazing practice. A couple of weeks later, he came into my office with an upbeat affect and demeanor. Rick shared with me how he had used the sky gazing practice during his morning break. By pausing and surrendering his problems to nature, he was able to just sit with his life condition, open up to possibility, and let the wisdom and lessons of nature speak to him. Sitting in this open way, Rick saw a vine on a tree that had been snipped away by a gardener. *But the vine started growing again.* In that moment, Rick had a powerful insight and realization of his own nature: He was resilient and wouldn't stop growing even if he lost his business—any more than a vine would just give up and die because a gardener snipped away at it. This epiphany spoke deeply to him about who he really was deep down, and he used that inner strength to reinvigorate and re-inspire him with newfound hope and purpose.

Whatever relationship struggles anyone endures, surrendering the rational mind and letting go of trying to "fix" things can sometimes be more helpful and healing to the spirit. This *Letting It Be with Sky Gazing* practice invites a deep acceptance, one in which nature plays an important role.

TIPS FOR WORKING WITH CLIENTS

Explore the idea of deep acceptance and surrender with clients. It may help to review ideas explored in Tip #1, *P.A.I.R. U.P. for Mindful Relationships*, about cultivating acceptance.

✓ Remind clients about the difference between surrender and submission.

- Surrender is a choice, and while it may not alter the situation, it may open one to a deeper understanding.

✓ Consider bundling together the following related practices:

- Tool 16, *Open the Compassionate Heart*
- Tool #21, *The Power of Acceptance and Patience*
- Tool #41, *Forest Bathing Meditation*

Letting It Be with Sky Gazing

Life often means having to deal with the impossible or unchangeable. Maybe you lost someone close to you, or maybe you endured a health issue that dramatically altered your life and relationships. There may be a way, however, to find a sense of peace.

It is called surrender. This is not to be confused with submission—which means you give up because you have no choice. Surrender is different, because it's a way of coming to peace when there are no easy answers. Surrendering lets you move forward in a different way, beyond rational thought.

Instructions

Find a quiet place in nature with a view of the sky. You can stand or sit during this practice, but make sure you won't be interrupted for up to 10 minutes. You can always continue for a longer period of time if you want.

Settle into the Body and Breath

Get settled in with a few nice diaphragmatic breaths. Notice the preciousness of each breath, how unique and special each one is. Take this next breath as if it were all that mattered to you right now.

Feel the body just as it is. This body, which comes from an ancient past, represents the accumulation of generations of wisdom. Tune into it now.

Center with a Prayer, Affirmation, or Mantra

Your centering intention here is not to solve or resolve your problem, but to go *beyond* your problem. To just rest the mind in a place of quiet surrender to the larger process.

Use any meaningful prayer, affirmation, or mantra to center and rest the mind. One prayer of peace and surrender is the Serenity Prayer:

> *God grant me the serenity*
> *To accept the things I cannot change;*
> *Courage to change the things I can;*
> *And the wisdom to know the difference.*

Cast Your Gaze Skyward

Look upward into the vastness. Have a soft gaze as you look into the sky, staying open. Eyes open, mind open, skin open, body open, ears open, every cell in the body open.

Release Your Personal Pain and Suffering without Expectation

As you Sky Gaze, release your worries into the vast, empty space above and beyond. With each exhale, release more, just letting it be.

Let the sky absorb and hold all your troubles. Release it all, let go of holding on and trying to change or fix it.

Surrender it now to the infinite vastness of the universe, which possesses a wisdom and meaning beyond our capabilities to understand. And that's okay. Just sit with the unknowable, unfathomable nature of things that are beyond the rational mind's need to know and control.

Rest in the Natural State of Interbeing

As you sit, continue to breathe, letting the separation between you and nature dissolve.

Know that the sky you see is also present in your eyes.

Feel how the clouds that produce the water you drink become part of your body.

Marvel at how the particles from the universe's beginning also formed your own cells.

Just sit. Letting it be. Surrendering to the sky. And beyond.

Open

As you open and surrender, make yourself available to whatever message or wisdom comes to you. This could be a feeling or knowing that is beyond words and which is felt in the body or elsewhere. It could be a flash of insight or awareness that comes to you in words or images. Or, you might just sit in silence. Whatever happens, you can know that it's all the blessing of this present moment. That not having to know is its own kind of relief, as well as a blessing.

Follow-Up

Consider journaling your experiences. Share this with others if you are comfortable doing so. Even if what happened in the moment can't be re-created—and that's okay—you can still remember the sense of truth, peace, wisdom, blessing, or whatever it was that you felt in that moment.

Tool #43 | The All-Purpose Nature Transition

Mindful Learning Styles

The following learning styles are compatible with this practice:

Visual-Spatial

Sound-Musical

Bodily-Kinesthetic-Tactile

Social-Interpersonal

Reflective-Intrapersonal

Natural World

THOUGHTS FOR THERAPISTS

Transitions can be difficult to navigate. It is during transitional times that we are prone to anxiety. That makes sense in terms of brain science because the part of the brain that triggers the fight or flight response—the amygdala—is receiving input from all our senses as we move about. While the amygdala is just doing its job, the problem is that the stress that accumulates as we go from one place to another often remains with us—such as when coming home after a stress-filled day at work. Since no one wants to take that stress out on the ones they care about, a calming transitional practice makes a lot of sense. Being aware of transitions is important, and Tool #29, *Rituals for Coming and Going*, examined ways that partners and others can use a ritual either before or after a transition. The tool here is about how to effectively transition by using nature to discharge negative stress.

One study showed that drivers who watched a pre-recorded video of a scenic drive as viewed through a car window felt calmer and less frustrated than when watching a video that depicted a drive through an urban setting.[50] Since drivers need to keep their eyes on the road, another suggestion is to take a short nature transition before heading home.

But just because someone takes a nice walk doesn't mean there can't still be issues. For example, we all know that Henry David Thoreau spent a lot of time in the woods. It must have been wonderfully idyllic, right? So you may be surprised by the frank admission shared in his essay *Walking*, published in *The Atlantic* magazine over 150 years ago. He wrote, "But it sometimes happens that I cannot easily shake off the village. The thought of some work will run in my head, and I am not where my body is—I am out of my senses…What business have I in the woods, if I am thinking of something out of the woods?"[51]

I think it's safe to say that Thoreau didn't have the distraction of a smart phone, and yet his attention still wandered off. That's why, in order to control mind wandering, we're going to add the very intentional practice of mindful walking to being in nature. In fact, one study demonstrated that the practice of integrating mindful walking and nature was an effective means of maintaining mindfulness skills.[52]

---

50 Jack Nasar, Natural scenes calm drivers more than city views, *Environment and Behavior,* Nov. 2003.

51 Henry David Thoreau, "Walking," https://www.theatlantic.com/magazine/archive/1862/06/walking/304674/ (accessed May 2017).

52 R.A. Gotink, K.S. Hermans, N. Geschwind, et al., *Mindfulness*, 2016; 7: 1114. https://doi.org/10.1007/s12671-016-0550-8.

TIPS FOR WORKING WITH CLIENTS

If clients are transitioning from work to home, find a nature setting near their home. Even a walk at a park, around the block, or in the backyard will work. Here are some other ideas to consider:

✓ Practice mindful walking around the office if possible. Or, have the client do this at home in a controlled environment before trying it in nature.

✓ Make sure all electronic gear is stowed away, kept in the car, or turned off. The pull of wanting to check messages or texts can be a major distraction and foil the purpose of this calm transition practice.

✓ This practice is helpful not just for transition, but as a contemplative practice or a way to just slow down and get centered when things feel overwhelming.

✓ Consider integrating this practice together with these other transitional tools:

- Tool #29, *Rituals for Coming and Going*
- Tool #33, *One-Minute Technology and Workplace Vacation*
- Tool #40, *Spontaneous Play*

The All-Purpose Nature Transition

Did you ever notice that when you transition from one place to another—such as getting to an appointment, going to the airport for a flight, or making a trip to the mall—that your anxiety level goes up? And if you're not careful, you might even bring bad stress home with you after a stressful day on the job.

If your stress is affecting your relationships, you might want to consider this practice—alone or with a partner. With another, this offers a nice way to attain a shared awareness of a slower, gentle pace.

In addition, walking in a natural setting can help discharge negative stress so that it doesn't have to be passed on to those you care about.

Instructions

Make sure to turn off your phone and stow any electronic devices where you won't be tempted to look at them or use them.

Find a place in nature where you can walk for 10 minutes, even longer. This can even be done in your backyard, down the street, at a park, or anywhere that it's quiet and where you can see nature. Ten minutes is recommended because it might take that long until your body actually slows down.

Breathe

Are you noticing a theme here? Most of the contemplative practices begin by taking two or three calming breaths because that's how you turn on the body's relaxation response and slow everything down. Keep some awareness on your breath even as you walk.

Intentionally Move and Walk

Mindful walking is an intentional practice. Whenever you do anything intentionally, it means that you're not just doing it by habit or mindlessly. Here, you'll be walking with a sense of purpose, making each step and movement in a deliberate way.

Simply, mindful walking consists of the following three-step process:

- Step 1 (Intention): Mentally set the intention to take a step.
- Step 2 (Action): Follow up by taking the step.
- Step 3 (Observe): Notice how your foot rises off the ground, moves through the air, how the heel and foot come down, and how your weight shifts from one side of the body to the other.

Note: By the way, if the above method doesn't feel natural to you, just allow yourself to flow, moving the body like a surfer becoming one with a wave or a skier moving as one with the slopes.

Special Note: *Mindful walking may slow down the pace, so if your balance is compromised, move at a pace at which you feel safe and stable! Even walking at a normal pace is okay so long as you are present with your movements.*

Pause to Notice Nature

Remember to stop for a few moments to observe nature. Let yourself feel the rhythm of the nature around you. Allow yourself to move with the same kind of flow and ease. Most importantly, because this practice takes you off autopilot mode, you will take each step as if you have never taken a step before.

Reflections

What was it like to walk in this way? What was most challenging about it for you? What was easiest?

_____

_____

_____

_____

_____

How long did it take until you really slowed down each step? How did this affect your balance? Did your mind stay focused on the intentional movement?

_____

_____

_____

_____

_____

How could you integrate this practice into your day? What would that look like?

_____

_____

_____

_____

_____

What is one way this practice could benefit you or others?

_____

_____

_____

_____

_____

Tool #44 | Rearrange Your Space & Relationships

Mindful Learning Styles

The following learning styles are compatible with this practice:

- Verbal-Linguistic
- Visual-Spatial
- Sound-Musical
- Bodily-Kinesthetic-Tactile
- Mathematical-Science-Logical

- Social-Interpersonal
- Reflective-Intrapersonal
- Natural World
- Existential-Meaning

THOUGHTS FOR THERAPISTS

In *The Feeling of What Happens*, neuroscientist Antonio Damasio wrote, "…the states of the living organism, within body bounds, are continuously being altered by encounters with objects or events in its environment, or, for that matter, by thoughts and by internal adjustments of the life process."[53] In other words, it's hard to separate the body we inhabit from the environment in which we move around!

Mindfulness is more than being aware of our inner world of thoughts, emotions, and physical sensations. Since we're wired for empathy, mindfulness has a bearing on our relationships. But mindfulness is also very much about our broader relationship with the total environment around us—from the entire eco-system down to the spatial and physical relationship we have with our living space at home and at work.

One client who came to see me, Victor, felt angry and pressured while at work. In fact, his metaphor for the workplace was that it was a "war zone." As I later learned through questioning, Victor's workspace had no windows. It was barren except for various schedulers, timeline charts, and computer terminals that kept him marching and keeping on task like a soldier. After having him alter his space—by bringing in plants, photos of open spaces, and personal photos—his metaphor changed and he was less depressed. Another client I worked with who faced a similar problem ended up bringing a fish tank into his workplace. He discovered it helped give him a sense of "flow" and peace while at work. Looking at the fish for even a few moments comforted and soothed him.

Of course, our wisdom traditions have long used beautiful imagery and structures to engender a feeling of spaciousness, transcendence, and awe. In the same way, rearranging our space is like growing and cultivating a garden. How we decorate and arrange our living areas can give us a sense of freedom and flow, or it can sap energy and feel suffocating. In this sense, the space that one inhabits can almost be imagined as the very real extension of the body itself.

---

[53] Antonio Damasio, *The Feeling of What Happens* (Wilmington, MA: Mariner Books, 2000), p. 30.

TIPS FOR WORKING WITH CLIENTS

If there are relational problems, explore the current living space arrangements. How might this be contributing, if at all, to the current issues? Some people are more sensitive to spatial needs and requirements. When considering potential changes, review Tip #3, *Identifying and Implementing Mindful Learning Styles.*

✓ Remember that any changes to a living space can be undone. This is just an experiment to see how it feels when a space is changed or transformed.

✓ To help clients get more tuned into the body and their needs, bundle this tool with the following:
  • Tool #12, *Body Regulation for Grounding and Attention*
  • Tool #18, *Stand Up and Know Your Needs*
  • Tool #30, *Imagine Your Joyful Next Chapter*, which could be used in this particular case to imagine *Your Joyful Living Space.*

Rearrange Your Space and Relationships

Did you ever stop to think about how certain environments make you feel? Your work or home environment might even be affecting your relationships.

This can be done alone and with another—with both persons filling out their answers and then mutually and respectfully exploring all the ideas.

Instructions

PART 1 — *Reconnect with Nature*

For a few moments think about a place in nature that you love. Imagine all the things you find pleasant about the place: The colors, the objects, the sounds, the shapes, the smells, the textures, the brightness, the darkness, and the types of patterns. Also, include things you like that are related to spatial shape, such as tall, short, narrow, wide, expansive, and broad. Write these all down below:

_____

_____

_____

_____

_____

_____

_____

Rearrange Your Living Space (Home, Work, Other)

Choose a space that you'd like to rearrange. Then, refer back to the comments above to help you as you decide how to rearrange your space. This is just an exercise, and you don't really have to move anything. So allow yourself to freely change your existing space.

Using your ideas from nature, answer these questions on a separate sheet of paper:

- How could I create a more peaceful and comfortable space?
- What would create openness and spaciousness?
- How would others feel about moving things around?
- How would my home look if arranged differently?
- What would it feel like to have a fresher arrangement?
- What fears, worries, and concerns do I have about rearranging?
- What would it be like to rearrange just for the sake of rearranging?
- What would I move first?

- What pieces would be most difficult to move (physically and/or emotionally)?
- Would I need some new furniture to do this?
- How long would the process take? How long could I allow it to take?
- What would be the possible advantages of rearranging?
- What would be the possible disadvantages?
- What are the expectations I place on rearranging?
- What is the best/worst that would happen by rearranging?

PART 2 — *Rearrange Your Relationship (Partner, Work, Other)*

Now that you've rearranged a "space," let's see what it would be like to rearrange some aspects of home or work relationships. Again, this is just an exercise and you don't really have to rearrange or change anything. So allow yourself to freely consider how you might change any existing relationship. Then, feel what that might be like.

- How could I create a more peaceful and comfortable relationship?
- What would create openness and spaciousness in the relationship?
- What would others feel about my rearranging the relationship?
- How would my relationship feel and look if arranged differently?
- What would it feel like to have a fresher relationship?
- What fears, worries, and concerns do I have about rearranging the relationship?
- What would it be like to rearrange the relationship just for the sake of rearranging?
- What would be hardest thing to rearrange in the relationship?
- What would I change first?
- What aspects would be most difficult to change (emotionally)?
- Would I need help to rearrange this relationship?
- How long would the process take? How long could I allow it to take?
- What would be the possible advantages of rearranging my relationship?
- What would be the possible disadvantages of rearranging it?
- What expectations do I place on changing my relationship?
- What is the best/worst that would happen by rearranging?

Reflections

What did you discover about your willingness to rearrange your living space and relationship? What is the connection between these for you?

_____

_____

_____

_____

How could the process of rearranging your living space also change your relationship?

_____

_____

_____

_____

What would have to happen for you to begin rearranging—both your living space and relationship—in ways that would give you greater peace, confidence, and safety? What would be your next step?

_____

_____

_____

_____

What one small step could you take this week (rearranging your living space or relationship) that could produce a positive result in your life?

_____

_____

_____

_____

Tool #45 | Nature's Relationship Repair Kit

Mindful Learning Styles

The following learning styles are compatible with this practice:

- Verbal-Linguistic
- Visual-Spatial
- Sound-Musical
- Bodily-Kinesthetic-Tactile
- Social-Interpersonal
- Reflective-Intrapersonal
- Natural World

THOUGHTS FOR THERAPISTS

One of the first studies to look at the link between nature and healing was the 1984 study conducted by environmental psychologist Roger Ulrich.[54] The study found that patients recovering from surgery who had a view of nature recovered significantly faster than patients whose room looked out on a brick wall. That work has been expanded, and hospital gardens are no longer peripheral to healing and health. Residential psychiatric treatment centers, for example, now routinely incorporate natural spaces filled with natural stones, sculptures, and water treatments. Over the years, a body of research has accumulated to show that the calming parasympathetic nervous system (see Tool #13, *Breath Regulation for Managing Stress*) is activated by nature.

In other words, nature calms down the brain's stress initiator and reactivity center—the amygdala. But imagine a relationship in crisis or in the aftermath of an argument, and with both partners' emotional fire alarms still blaring! It's hard to repair the damage at that time because the thinking part of the brain—the frontal cortex—has gone offline like a computer hard drive that has just crashed. While diaphragmatic breathing can bring the thinking brain back online, nature accomplishes this in an even more elegant and powerful way.

Nature dramatically shifts the context of place and time. In addition to soothing and calming the brain, nature removes the old environmental triggers and habitual ways of thinking and acting that partners under distress typically encounter. In fact, one study found that when exposed to nature, subjects were more compassionate and generous.[55] If you want to foster a loving and compassionate brain, think nature.

---

[54] Roger Urich, View through a window may influence recovery from surgery, *Science*, 1984, Apr 27; 224(4647): 420–421.

[55] Netta Weinstein, Andrew Przybylski, et. al., Can nature make us more caring? Effects of immersion in nature on intrinsic aspirations and generosity, *Personality and Social Psychology Bulletin*, 2009; 35(10): 1315–1329.

TIPS FOR WORKING WITH CLIENTS

Find out how clients have used nature in the past. How comfortable are they with nature? What setting has made them feel most safe and calm?

✓ Consider using this with other nature tools such as:
- Tool #41, *Forest Bathing Meditation*
- Tool #43, *The All-Purpose Nature Transition*, for walking mindfully in nature.
- Tool #48, *Tending Your Relationship Garden*
- Tool #49, *Seasons of Nature; Seasons of Relationships*

Nature's Relationship Repair Kit

For those times that a relationship is in a rut or when you've had a disagreement with someone and still have hard feelings, one possible way to move forward and repair things is by using nature.

Nature has been shown to have properties that make us calmer and even enhance feelings of kindness and caring. If you feel stuck, this handout might offer a positive way to shift toward a new mindset. This handout is something that both partners do together.

Instructions

Look at the steps below. You will go through this *in advance* and make decisions together about where and when to go to nature. This way, you won't have to think about it when feeling upset. You will already know exactly what to do.

Step 1 — *Openness and Willingness*

For this to work, it's important in advance that each partner be willing to try this nature repair. Answer the following questions together: How have strategies for repairing arguments or issues worked for you in the past? Would it be worth trying a new strategy? What's the worst that could happen? What's the best that could happen?

_____

_____

_____

Step 2 — *Agree on a Nature Setting*

What nature setting is easy to get to that you and another both like? Ideally this would be a place where you can walk. Alternatively, you might also agree to visiting each other's favorite nature setting. Write down your top three places to visit that are within 10–20 minutes away. If you have a favorite place that is further away, how could you make that work without too much advance planning?

_____

_____

_____

Step 3 — *Pre-arranged Travel Kit*

Before you even go, what things would you like to take with you? You can put anything you want in your "Travel Kit," such as something to eat, a blanket for sitting on, hiking or walking shoes, a ball, a

Frisbee, etc. The idea here is that you will have these items all together and ready to go at a moment's notice. Write down what you'd like to take with you.

_____

_____

_____

Step 4 — *When to Go?*

How will you know the time is right for you and another to make the nature trip? This is for the two of you to decide. You might decide that either partner can make the decision if they feel it would be useful. You might decide that certain behavior means you need to take the trip. You know these trigger points better than anyone, so write your thoughts below.

_____

_____

_____

Step 5 — *Repair Process Takes Time*

Once you're in nature, it will take time for nature to work its magic. The time you are in nature is NOT the time to revisit or repeat the argument or disagreement that took place earlier. You will have time for that later. The purpose of nature is to help you get calm, grow softer, and to reconnect in a more mindful and compassionate way with the one you are with.

If, while in nature, you happen to feel that you can speak in a more compassionate way and without anger, then you may decide to do so. In the space below, write down your agreement to allow nature to be healing. After nature has calmed and soothed, how do you see a conversation or other relationship repair occurring?

_____

_____

_____

Step 6 — *Take Several Practice Runs*

What will you do in nature? How long will feel right until you settle in and feel calmer, more at ease, and playful? What activities work best? The best way—maybe the only way—to find out what works best is to take several "practice runs" by going out and putting into practice everything you've written here. You may decide you need to revise what's in your "Pre-arranged Travel Kit." Add further thoughts about practicing here.

_____

_____

_____

Review and Revise

Once you've actually experienced nature in the way described above, feel free to make changes. You will learn what works best for you and others. Above all, be flexible and adaptable as you apply these ideas.

Tool #46 | Two-getherness at Mealtime

THOUGHTS FOR THERAPISTS

There may be nothing more nature-connected and intimate than the simple act of appreciating the food that nature provides, as well as sharing a meal with others. The use of technology, however, has dramatically changed how we experience mealtime. Since the advent of television in the 1950s, the time-honored "family circle" around the dinner table got broken open and replaced with TV trays. Later, the microwave and fast food preparation further disjointed the family meal. Eating became sequential—as family members individually came into the kitchen, quickly ate, and then left the scene faster than a hit-and-run driver. Is it possible to once again reclaim the family mealtime circle?

If you're even wondering if it matters, there is a lot of new research demonstrating some surprising benefits of having a dedicated family meal. For children in a family, these include such things as improved grades, higher resilience, and a reduced risk of substance abuse, teen pregnancy, and depression.[56]

By creating an island of peace at mealtime, families and relationships make the statement that this is a time for us, for two-getherness (or three-getherness, as the case may be). It is a time to reconnect, to revalue, and reassess the day with others. A lot has been written about eating in a more enlightened way, such as *The Zen of Eating* by Ronna Kabatznick, *The Joy of Half a Cookie* by Jean Kristeller and Alisa Bowman, *Mindful Eating* by Jan Chozen Bays, and my own *Art of the Inner Meal*—which delves into how our major wisdom traditions use food practices as a pathway for deeper spiritual meaning and awakening. Mealtime creates a relationship ritual that is as meaningful as it is sustaining. Most importantly, preparing food, eating, and cleaning up afterwards models how we can work and live together with thoughtfulness, caring, and joy.

TIPS FOR WORKING WITH CLIENTS

As always, one's history around mealtime can be telling. If the family mealtime was stressful and inconsistent, this might be an opportunity for creating new, healthy, and beneficial patterns.

---

[56] "Benefits of Family Dinners," https://thefamilydinnerproject.org/about-us/benefits-of-family-dinners/ (accessed May 2017).

✓ Combine *Two-getherness at Mealtime* with the following practices that could be incorporated as a mealtime practice:

- Tool #26, *Enhance Relationships with a Positive Shared Memory*, by sharing a memory at the mealtime.

- Tool #27, *Identifying Strengths to Build Closeness*, by sharing something about the strength of another.

- Tool #37, *Softening with G.L.A.D.*, by sharing one's G.L.A.D. experiences of the day.

Two-getherness at Mealtime

Mealtime offers an opportunity to establish a sense of togetherness. It's the perfect time to share experiences of the day and to offer positive messages to those around you. However you may have experienced mealtime in the past, you can create a nurturing ritual of your own.

Here are some suggestions for elevating any mealtime from the mundane and ordinary into the realm of the special and extraordinary.

Instructions

The ideas below are just suggestions, so pick the ones you like best. As with any practice, consistency is important, so even if you do this once or twice a week, you can make that your special mealtime.

Create an Island of Peace

To make mealtime a true island of peace, remove technology and distractions such as:

- Turn off all phones so there is no texting or checking devices.
- Avoid watching TVs, computers, and other distractions.
- Leave enough time for talking before and after the meal.

Beautify and Invite in Nature

What would make this meal a little more special? What natural elements, such as scents and sounds can add to your meal? Some ideas include:

- Flowers
- Plants
- Candles
- Soft lighting
- Soothing music
- Special table setting
- Eating outside when possible

Mindfully Select and Prepare the Food

Allow extra time to prepare the meal in an unrushed way. Choose foods that are nutritious and wholesome, and containing as few processed ingredients as possible. Work together as a team to prepare the meal.

Start with a Mealtime Blessing

There are many books filled with different kinds of mealtime blessings. Even a moment of silence before the meal is a good way for centering. If desired, take turns saying the blessing.

Share Something Positive During the Meal

There are many ways to share something positive from the day's experiences. Consider having each person share one of the following:

- One thing of gratitude that was noticed.
- One delightful occurrence that made you smile.
- The G.L.A.D. experiences of the day (Tool #37, *Softening with G.L.A.D.*).
- One kind thing that happened.
- One thing to appreciate about each person at the dinner table.

Conclude with a Moment of Appreciation or Silence

Transitioning out of mealtime is often forgotten. Whether holding hands or sitting for a moment in silence, you acknowledge that this meal was special.

Finally, mindfully share in the clean-up.

Reflections

What would be the most challenging thing about creating this kind of a mealtime with your partner and others? What is the easiest thing about it? If you haven't done this kind of a meal in a while, how could you start?

_____

_____

_____

_____

What is one positive thing that could come from creating an island of peace around mealtime for your relationships? Even if you did this for yourself, what one positive thing could come from it?

_____

_____

_____

_____

Tool #47 | Attune to Nature's Pace

THOUGHTS FOR THERAPISTS

I'll never forget the day I was teaching a class at Lewis and Clark College Graduate School of Education and Counseling. It was a glorious, sunny and breezy day, and so I decided to introduce an outdoor mindfulness practice. Students were instructed to go outside—where there was a large grassy field, a rose garden, and several trees—and attune themselves with the pace of nature. The idea was to get everyone to slow down and get immersed in nature's mysteries by bringing a childlike awareness to whatever unique and novel thing caught their attention.

When we returned inside after 20 minutes, I heard some wonderful experiences. But most memorable was the story of a student who noticed a worm moving through the grass at a very, very, slow pace, as you'd expect with a worm. She told us, "I got down on my hands and knees so I could watch the worm. It would turn a little bit to the right or left, and I started wondering, which way is it going to turn next? I got so engrossed that I watched that worm for the whole 20 minutes and couldn't keep my eyes off it! It was the most amazing worm."

What was incredible and extraordinary to me was that she had literally attuned with her natural surroundings. How else could she have had the patience—worm-like patience, might I add—to focus on something without sensing frustration, impatience, or boredom, and without wanting to be somewhere else? She was one with the worm!

This happens because there's nothing phony or artificial about nature. It's not concocted like a theme park or a video game designed to get us addicted through adrenaline and rewards. Nature teaches by virtue of being authentic and real. It has no agenda, and when we attune with it, we get a glimpse of what authenticity, patience, perseverance, and resilience really are. *An acorn doesn't try to be an oak. An oak tree doesn't want to be skinny like a palm tree.*

This says a lot about the wisdom of letting our partners and others be who they are, without trying to mold them into our idea of a being a better oak tree or palm tree!

TIPS FOR WORKING WITH CLIENTS

For those persons who struggle with developing patience, paying attention to nature and attuning with this tool might provide for a fresh perspective.

✓ For those clients who like a nature and contemplative approach, try these related handouts:
  - Tool #41, *Forest Bathing Meditation*
  - Tool #43, *The All-Purpose Nature Transition*
  - Tool #48, *Tending Your Relationship Garden*

Attune to Nature's Pace

There's an interesting Zen saying that goes like this:

Sitting quietly,

doing nothing,

spring comes,

and the grass grows by itself.

How effortless that sounds. What incredible patience a blade of grass must have. Could things really be that natural? Maybe they could be, if only we learned to attune with the natural world. To move at the pace of nature means that we could accept where we are right now. Imagine if an acorn wanted to be a fully mature oak tree by tomorrow. What frustration and impatience and suffering it would experience!

Nature illustrates the importance of rhythm and pace, and the value of taking things one step at a time. Attuning with nature can cultivate a deeper understanding and acceptance for not worrying about things over which we have no control, as well as the people over whom we have no control.

Try this practice alone, or with a partner, and then compare notes.

Instructions

Set aside 20 minutes to do this practice. Do this practice when you won't feel pressured by other obligations. It's important that you recognize that only by allowing enough time can you experience this attunement.

Be Present with Nature's Rhythm

This is unlike the other nature practices because you are looking for the way nature moves.

Notice the flow, the effort, the rhythm, the pace, the patience, the persistence, the tenacity, and the purposefulness.

Maybe you will see a bee as it weaves through the air or a worm arching slowly through the grass. Watch how leaves dance in the breeze.

Just observe. With full presence for as long as you want. What must that be like to move or be like that?

Breathe with Nature

Allow your breath to come into the cadence of nature surrounding you. Let it move you, rather than you moving it. There's nothing to force. Come to peace with the breath just as it is, effortless and light, just like the sun that shines and the leaf that absorbs the sunlight.

Move as Nature

Although we are mammals, we can mimic other forms of nature. So now, have fun and allow yourself to move like the nature around you.

Let your body stretch as your arms reach up to the sky like a tall tree. Roll on the grass like your cat if you want! Move like the gentle breeze. Let your feet feel the earth, the ground. Continue to move in this way for as long as you want.

Be Real as Nature

Say what you will about nature, one thing is for certain. It's real, authentic, and not trying to be anything else. A tree makes no pretenses about wanting to be taller or thinner than it is. Neither does it get impatient for spring so its buds can finally appear. There is no wanting, no craving.

This is deep peace. Total unlimited patience.

It's the peace of taking the next breath without even trying.

Not a worry. It all gets done.

And springtime still comes.

And the grass still grows by itself.

Be Strong as Nature

Without even trying nature has a quiet persistence, strength, and resilience. As is written in the Tao:

The softest waters carve the hardest stone.

Notice and attune with the strength of nature. Notice it in the big things and the smallest of things. Now, sense your own strength.

Reflections

After you spend time in nature, journal your experience. You might want to share this with someone close to you. Or, use these reflections to explore. What did you notice by attuning with nature in these ways?

_____

_____

_____

_____

What would it be like to attune with nature in your relationship? How would things be different?

_____

_____

_____

_____

How did it feel to move at the pace of nature? How could this change your attitudes about patience and acceptance?

_____

_____

_____

_____

What wisdom or lessons could you take from nature that speak to your own strength, resilience, persistence, and tenacity?

_____

_____

_____

_____

_____

Tool #48	# Tending Your Relationship Garden

THOUGHTS FOR THERAPISTS

Back when I worked in an intensive outpatient eating disorder clinic, I sometimes asked clients—who suffered from anorexia or bulimia symptoms—to find a plant that they could care for. As someone who doesn't have a green thumb, I've learned that my indoor plants need to be watched. They need to get the proper amount of light. They need the right amount of water—not too much and not too little. And, they require the right kind of soil, nutrients, and enough space to grow. Properly cared for, plants will thrive and flower as nature intends. For many of the patients who started caring for a plant of their own, this message resonated with their own life and behavior. The metaphor of tending to our relationships in this way is suggested by the following poem:

> *Each Spring I plant a friendship field*
> *with seeds of loving-kindness.*
> *Every day I nurture my field*
> *with caring words, actions, joys, and hopes.*
> *I water it often with compassion and laughter.*
> *Come harvest time my field overflows,*
> *with enough friendship to warm and sustain me,*
> *during even the darkest, coldest winter.*[57]

Metaphors like this, whether illustrated by using an actual plant, a poem, or just the idea of a relationship as a garden, can sometimes provide a visual and very sensory-oriented roadmap for how to respond and act. Research shows, for example, that metaphor does more than just light up parts of the brain related to language and comprehension. It also activates the sensory areas of the brain.[58] In this way metaphor adds depth and real "feel" to its message.

---

[57] Donald Altman, *Friendship Field*, Mindful Eating Meal Cards, Portland, OR: Moon Lake Media, 2007.

[58] "Metaphors actually trigger the sensory parts of our brains," http://io9.gizmodo.com/5883554/metaphors-actually-trigger-the-sensory-parts-of-our-brains (accessed May 2017).

TIPS FOR WORKING WITH CLIENTS

With this particular metaphor, it might be interesting to see if the client has a personal background with plants. That's not necessary, since we all understand how plants need certain requirements to thrive.

Consider bundling the following tools together. All include different ways of tending a relationship, such as through intention, play, focused attention, loving-kindness, and compassion.

✓ Tool #16, *Open the Compassionate Heart*

✓ Tool #24, *S.T.O.P. the Relationship Robot of Reactivity*

✓ Tool #25, *Using Affirmations as a Relationship GPS*

✓ Tool #27, *Identifying Strengths to Build Closeness*

✓ Tool #35, *The Gift of Forgiveness*

✓ Tool #40, *Spontaneous Play*

✓ Tool #46, *Two-getherness at Mealtime*

Three Steps to Tending Your Relationship Garden

Did you ever care for a plant? Even if you haven't, you know that plants require the right amount of light, water, nutrients from the soil, and enough space to take root and grow. When you think about it, relationships have similar needs. But if they don't get the proper attention, love, caring, compassion, play, and so on, they can get in a rut and slowly wither on the vine, so to speak.

Even if a relationship—or plant for that matter—is struggling, the proper care will renew and rejuvenate it.

Instructions

Read the poem that follows, then look at the steps for tending your own relationship garden.

Each Spring I plant a friendship field
with seeds of loving-kindness.
Every day I nurture my field
with caring words, actions, joys, and hopes.
I water it often with compassion and laughter.
Come harvest time my field overflows,
with enough friendship to warm and sustain me,
during even the darkest, coldest winter.

Step 1 — *Seed Your Garden with Kind Speech and Intentions*

Intentions are like the seeds that, once planted and watered, grow into mature plants. Are your intentions for the relationship coming from your own selfish desires? Or, are they oriented toward what you can give to another—respect, understanding, acceptance, compromise, etc.—thus including the "We" perspective?

Likewise, is your speech kind and loving, in both tone and content? Harsh, unkind, and spiteful words are not easily forgotten, and they are just the kind of thing that can keep any relationship from flowering and thriving.

In the space below, write down the positive intentions you can start planting. Also, write down your intention to use kind speech, along with a description of what that would look like.

_____

_____

_____

_____

Step 2 — *Water Your Garden with Daily Actions of Love, Generosity and Laughter*

The love and laughter you demonstrate each day keeps your relationship alive and growing. What's more, by depositing more laughter into your relationship "bank," you build up a buffer of good will that can counterbalance the challenges. How do you lighten up your relationship? Is your time with another focused on the complaints of life? Surely, it's okay to rant every now and then—but even rants can be done in a spirit of fun.

In the space below, honestly assess the attitude, generosity, and lightness you bring into your relationship. How could you bring in more sunshine and sprinkle the relationship with loving touches to keep it engaged, joyous, and alive?

_____

_____

_____

_____

Step 3 — *Feed Your Garden with the Nutrients of Understanding and Compassion*

There is perhaps no better way to tend and grow your relationship garden than to offer your compassion, understanding, and forgiveness. No one is perfect, and your partner must endure conditions in life that produce suffering. Given that knowledge, you can be the gardener who shields his or her plants from stormy and extreme weather. In the space below, write down some of the ways you can nurture your relationship with these special and enduring qualities.

_____

_____

_____

_____

Tool #49 | Seasons of Nature; Seasons of Relationships

Mindful Learning Styles

The following learning styles are compatible with this practice:

Verbal-Linguistic

Visual-Spatial

Mathematical-Science-Logical

Social-Interpersonal

Reflective-Intrapersonal

Natural World

Existential-Meaning

THOUGHTS FOR THERAPISTS

How often have you heard someone make a comment about a partner that went something like this: "I don't even recognize him anymore," or "She's not the same person I married," or "I don't know what happened. Everything was so perfect." And very likely, they are right. So what happened to that partner and relationship that changed so dramatically? One potential perspective for understanding change can be found through the lens of nature and the seasons.

The Lakota medicine man, or holy man, Black Elk spoke of the immutable and continuous nature of the seasons of life by sagely stating, "Even the seasons form a great circle in their changing, and always come back again to where they were. The life of a man is a circle from childhood to childhood, and so it is in everything where power moves."[59]

Just as the Earth cannot help but move through the seasons, relationships move through seasons in a similar way. There's springtime, brimming with energy, excitement, unlimited hope, and new love. There's summer, filled with the warm feelings of pleasure, planning, activity, and bliss. There is fall, a time of slowing down, letting things be, and finding contentment and appreciation. Finally, there's winter, with its need for quietude, reflection, and time to review dreams, hopes, and deal with loss.

It's important to recognize and appreciate each of these seasons for what they offer. Unlike the seasons of nature, however, these are not written in stone. No relationship will ever remain the same over time. Still, these seasons can serve as landmarks. By recognizing them, we can realize that maybe a relationship would benefit from a little more of the qualities of springtime, summer, fall, or winter. From a mindfulness approach, one season is not innately better than any other. We can experience them all, and appreciate what each has to offer.

---

[59] John Neihardt, *Black Elk Speaks* (Lincoln, NE: Bison Books, 2014), p. 121.

TIPS FOR WORKING WITH CLIENTS

Partners can each complete a handout separately, and then share their findings with one another.

✓ Consider bundling this practice with the following tools as a way to help partners understand and accept the dynamic and ever-changing nature of relationships.
- Tool #19, *Resilience and Sharing a Story of Hope*
- Tool #22, *Get C.U.R.I.O.U.S.*
- Tool #36, *Building Trust that Lasts*
- Tool #48, *Tending Your Relationship Garden*

What Is Your Relationship Season?

You know what season it is, but do you know what "season" your relationship is in?

Nature teaches us a lot about how things naturally change over time. For example, springtime is filled with new growth, energy, excitement, and hope—just like many new relationships. If someone you know has ever commented on how their relationship has drastically changed, then they've likely identified a new season without even knowing it.

When changes occur in a relationship, these may not necessarily be bad. It might mean that a relationship has entered another phase, or season. By understanding the seasons below, you'll have a better awareness and insight into your own relationship. Often, relationships start in springtime and go through the various seasons. But each relationship is unique.

Instructions

Look through each of the season descriptions here. Relationships are varied and unique, so your relationship season may have many or only a few of the qualities mentioned. Let your gut sense tell you what season your relationship is in.

Afterwards, answer the reflections and compare your findings with your partner.

Spring Relationship Season

Spring relationships are brimming with energy, excitement, hope, positivity, and new love. There might be a roller coaster of moods in this season, even feelings of insecurity and worry because you don't know how this particular "ride" will turn out. But there is also a lot of hope for the future. Your partner might seem so ideal that you can't believe your good luck! This is a time of sensuality, intimacy, romance, togetherness, and passion. This season often brings heightened feelings of positive emotions. This season is filled with "on the edge of your seat" anticipation for the joys you will find together.

Summer Relationship Season

Summer relationships have settled in. The roller coaster of emotions has been replaced by a less exciting, but safer and more secure ride. This season fills you with the warm feelings of pleasure, activity, planning, and love. Despite conflicts, there are still new things to experience. There are plans and goals and things to achieve. The relationship expands outward during this season, often inviting in new friends and family. It might seem like there's nothing you can't do this summer if you desire it!

Fall Relationship Season

Fall relationships mean that the tempo is slowing down. Conflicts and differences may appear larger, and there could be less activity, energy, and striving for new things—and romantic energy and emotions may have cooled down as well. For some, there might be a sense of comfort and ease with the way things are, as well as an attitude of contentment, appreciation, and peace. Partners might seek their own hobbies or paths to joy. This separateness might bring emotional coldness, sadness, or disappointment; for others, it could bring happiness, connectedness, and joy for one's partner.

Winter Relationship Season

Winter relationships are a time for quietude and reflection. Activity might feel like it's come to a standstill. There's little or no emotional energy left to expend, or there might be irrational emotional outbursts. Depending on life experiences related to loss, betrayal, and mistrust, there could be emotional coldness that leads to a review of the relationship's dreams and hopes. Health, financial loss, and emotional distance can bring doubt about the future. There might be the feeling that the relationship cannot survive this harsh season.

Reflections

After looking through the seasons above, what seasons has your relationship experienced so far? Have your seasons jumped around or happened one after the other?

_____

_____

_____

_____

What season seems to typify where you are at right now? How do you feel about this? What's the hardest thing about this season? What's the easiest?

_____

_____

_____

_____

A relationship that included something from all the different seasons would be a well-balanced one. What parts of other seasons would you borrow that could make your relationship stronger? What is one tangible action or thing that would help to do that?

_____

_____

_____

_____

No relationship season is innately good or bad. How can you grow from this current season, and how can that help you to move forward?

_____

_____

_____

_____

Tool #50	# Sun Breathing B.L.E.S.S. Meditation

Mindful Learning Styles

The following learning styles are compatible with this practice:

Verbal-Linguistic

Visual-Spatial

Sound-Musical

Bodily-Kinesthetic-Tactile

Social-Interpersonal

Natural World

THOUGHTS FOR THERAPISTS

When the group U2 sang "two hearts beating as one," anyone might think the phrase was just poetic license. After all, who knows how many songwriters have used those lyrics over the years? Believe it or not, research shows that there's a very real kernel of truth in those words. A study conducted by UC Davis had the partners of over 30 couples sit a few feet apart in a quiet room. What they found was that the couple's heart rates got in sync and that the pair even breathed at the same intervals. If you're thinking that might just happen to any two persons, the researchers tested for that as well. When two persons from different couples were seated together, there was no syncing of heart rate or respiration.[60]

While scientists aren't sure how this happens, it's evident that persons who are close get connected physiologically and emotionally. *The Sun Breathing B.L.E.S.S. Meditation* that follows is a soothing practice that will synchronize partners without their even being taught to do this—as was the case with Tool #20, *Self-Soothing and Synchronized Breathing*. This practice can be done with entire families or other groups of persons as well.

TIPS FOR WORKING WITH CLIENTS

This practice might be useful for clients who enjoy the out of doors. This could be used before or after a walk, or used with the following tools. It might naturally fit with Tool #45, *Nature's Relationship Repair Kit*.

- ✓ Tool #20, *Self-Soothing and Synchronized Breathing*
- ✓ Tool #28, *The Tenderness of Touch and Intimacy*
- ✓ Tool #40, *Spontaneous Play*
- ✓ Tool #45, *Nature's Relationship Repair Kit*

This is a meditative practice, so use the handout as a guided script to read during session. Then give the clients a handout, which they can follow along with later.

---

[60] J.L. Helm, D. Sbarra, et al., Assessing cross-partner associations in physiological responses via coupled oscillator models, *Emotion*, 2012 Aug; 12(4): 748–762. doi: 10.1037/a0025036. Epub 2011 Sep 12.

Sun Breathing B.L.E.S.S. Meditation

This meditation is a nice practice to do by yourself or with another. Also, it can be done either indoors or outside, whichever works best. You can be flexible in how you use this. You could do this briefly before or after a walk, in the morning or when you return from work, at night before bedtime. If you use it at night, you can call it a Moon Breathing Meditation!

Practice this a few times so you know it, and one person can lead you in the meditation. Or just read the words below as a guide.

Instructions

This is a meditation for finding peace within and with another. Begin by finding a quiet place in nature where you won't be interrupted. Or, you can do this in your own home looking out at nature or in any room.

Stand Tall like a Tree

To start, stand up with your feet firmly planted on the ground. Imagine yourself rooted and grounded like one of the trees before you, or one of your favorite trees. If you have a partner, stand side by side about five or six feet apart, but both looking in the same direction, facing nature.

Stand nice and tall, just like that tree. Now, follow along with the acronym B.L.E.S.S.

B — *Breathe*

This B means take some nice relaxed belly breaths. This is slow and rhythmic breathing. Don't try too hard. Just let the breath be easy, with no effort. Let the breath move your body, almost like the breeze that causes a tree to slightly sway and move.

Good, there's no rush. Now just bring awareness to how you are breathing with another. Each of you is sharing this precious moment, noticing the trees, and being with one another. You breathe the same air, you are rooted in the same ground. Let yourself feel how the earth and the air are also part of you. Now we will move on to the letter L in the B.L.E.S.S. acronym.

L — *Love*

The L stands for love. So right now, let yourself feel the heart center in your body as it opens up. And let it radiate and pour out the love of compassion for all living things. Let this healing, expansive love go throughout your own body, too, letting it absorb deeply into all your cells, from the bottom of your feet to your fingertips to the top of your head. You can also breathe in love from the earth beneath your feet. Allow that to come in, too.

Just stand for a few more moments, breathing and basking in the warm glow of love from within and without. Wonderful. Now let's move to the letter E.

E — *Elevate*

The E stands for elevate, as in slowly raise your arms upward with palms facing up. Like tree branches let your arms reach up until they settle in to comfortable height. Continue to breathe and warm yourself with love.

The E in elevate also means "elevate your view," as in imagine yourself high on a mountaintop with an unlimited view of the world below you. (You can close your eyes if you want to.) From this majestic point of view all the worries of the world seem smaller, and there is a feeling of spaciousness, wholeness, and completeness.

Just rest for a moment longer, absorbing the love that this world is capable of, and sensing all who make it a safer and more compassionate place. Wonderful!

Now let's move on to the first S in our B.L.E.S.S. acronym.

S — *Sun*

The S stands for sun, the light that illuminates and warms and makes life possible. Even if you are inside or cannot see the sun, close your eyes and imagine the warmth of the bright sun as it blankets your upward-facing palms with light and heat. Let your palms be like the leaves on a tree. Let this life-giving source energize and harmonize within you. Continue to feel the warm love radiating from your heart, as it mixes with the sun's energy, making you feel radiant, joyful, energized, and strong.

Still, be aware of the presence of your partner standing nearby as you both breathe in the sun and feel the radiance of joy from your elevated view.

S — *Sacredness*

The last S stands for sacredness, which is the sacredness of the body and mind—which you intimately experience. It's also the sacredness of the sun, the earth, the air, the sky, the world—that you can experience intimately, as part of you.

Very slowly, bring the hand that is closest to your partner down until your hands touch. Hold hands as you continue to breathe, feeling love from your heart now circulating and radiating not just into your own body, but into your partner's body. Feel and appreciate the sacredness between the two of you for a minute or so.

When you are done, bring your palms together in front of the heart center.

If you want, you can conclude this meditation by giving thanks for the blessings in your life. And you can make a commitment to reducing harm in all your relationships through offering compassion, understanding, and kindness.

Bibliography/Resources

BOOKS

Altman, Donald, *101 Mindful Ways to Build Resilience: Cultivate Calm, Clarity, Optimism & Happiness Each Day*, PESI Publishing and Media, 2016.

Altman, Donald, *Clearing Emotional Clutter: Mindfulness Practices for Letting Go of What's Blocking Your Fulfillment and Transformation*, New World Library, 2016.

Altman, Donald, *Stay Mindful & Color*, PESI Publishing and Media, 2016.

Altman, Donald, *The Mindfulness Toolbox: 50 Practical Tips, Tools, and Handouts for Anxiety, Depression, Stress, and Pain*, PESI Publishing and Media, 2014.

Altman, Donald, *The Joy Compass: 8 Ways to Find Lasting Happiness, Gratitude and Optimism in the Present Moment*, New Harbinger Publications, 2012.

Altman, Donald, *A Course in Mindfulness: The Heart of Mindful Living*, Moon Lake Media, 2011 (available at: www.MindfulPractices.com).

Altman, Donald, *One-Minute Mindfulness: 50 Simple Ways to Find Peace, Clarity and New Possibilities in a Stressed-Out World*, New World Library, 2011.

Altman, Donald, *Mindfulness Code: Keys for Overcoming Stress, Anxiety, Fear, and Unhappiness*, New World Library, 2010.

Altman, Donald, *Living Kindness: The Buddha's Ten Guiding Principles for a Blessed Life*, Moon Lake Media, 2009.

Altman, Donald, *Eat, Savor, Satisfy: 12-Weeks to Mindful Eating*, Moon Lake Media, 2006 (available at: www.MindfulPractices.com).

Altman, Donald, *Meal by Meal: 365 Daily Meditations for Finding Balance through Mindful Eating*, New World Library, 2004.

Altman, Donald, *Art of the Inner Meal: The Power of Mindful Practices to Heal Our Food Cravings*, Moon Lake Media, 2002.

Armstrong, Thomas, *7 Kinds of Smart: Identifying and Developing Your Multiple Intelligences*, Plume, 1999.

Baer, Ruth, *Mindfulness-Based Treatment Approaches*, Elsevier, 2006.

Baldoni, John, *MOXIE: The Secrets to Bold and Gutsy Leadership*, Routledge, 2014.

Baldoni, John, *Great Motivation Secrets of Great Leaders*, McGraw-Hill, 2005.

Barker, Philip, *Using Metaphors in Psychotherapy*, Bruner Meisel U., 1987.

Begley, Sharon, *Train Your Brain, Change Your Mind*, Ballantine Books, 2007.

Benson, Herbert, and Proctor, William, *Relaxation Revolution: The Science and Genetics of Mind Body Healing*, Scribner, 2011.

Biswas-Diener, Robert, *Invitation to Positive Psychology: Research and Tools for the Professional*, PositiveAcorn.com, 2008.

Bohm, David, *On Dialogue*, Routledge, 2004.

Bryant, Fred, and Veroff, Joseph, *Savoring: A New Model of Positive Experience*, Lawrence Erlbaum Associates, 2006.

Burns, David, *Feeling Good*, Harper & Row, 1980.

Butler, James, *Mindful Classrooms: 5-Minute Daily Mindfulness Practices to Empower Teachers and Students*, MindfulClassrooms.com, 2016.

Butler, James, *Mindfulness Is*, MindfulClassrooms.com, 2016.

Chödrön, Pema, *Start Where You Are: A Guide to Compassionate Living*, Shambala, 2001.

Craigie, Jr., Frederic, *Positive Spirituality in Health Care: Nine Practical Approaches to Pursuing Wholeness for Clinicians, Patients, and Health Care Organizations*, Mill City Press, 2010.

Daiensai, Richard Kirsten, *Smile: 365 Happy Meditations*, MQ Pub., Ltd., 2004.

Davidson, Richard, and Begley, Sharon, *The Emotional Life of Your Brain*, Plume, 2012.

Diener, Ed, and Biswas-Diener, Robert, *Happiness: Unlocking the Mysteries of Psychological Wealth*, Blackwell Publishing, 2008.

Flores, Philip, *Addiction as an Attachment Disorder*, Aronson, 2003.

Fralich, Terry, *Cultivating Lasting Happiness*, Premier Publishing Media, 2012.

Gershon, Michael, *The Second Brain*, Harper Paperbacks, 1999.

Hanson, Rick, *Buddha's Brain: The Practical Neuroscience of Happiness, Love and Wisdom*, New Harbinger Publications, 2009.

Hayes, Steven, and Smith, Spencer, *Get Out of Your Mind & Into Your Life*, New Harbinger Publications, 2005.

Hayes, Steven; Follette, Victoria; Linehan, Marsha; editors, *Mindfulness and Acceptance: Expanding the Cognitive Behavioral Tradition*, Guilford Press, 2004.

Hüther, Gerald, *The Compassionate Brain: How Empathy Creates Intelligence*, Trumpeter Books, 2006.

Jevne, R.F., and Miller, J.E., *Finding Hope: Ways to See Life in a Brighter Light*, Willowgreen Publishing, 1999.

Kabat-Zinn, Jon, *Wherever You Go, There You Are: Mindfulness Meditation in Everyday Life*, Hyperion Books, 1997.

Klein, Allen, *The Healing Power of Humor*, Tarcher Press, 1989.

Kornfield, Jack, *The Art of Forgiveness, Loving-Kindness, and Peace*, Bantam Books, 2002.

Lama, Dalai, *Beyond Religion: Ethics for a Whole World*, Mariner Books, 2012.

Lama, Dalai, *The Art of Happiness, 10th Anniversary Edition: A Handbook for Living*, Riverhead Books, 2009.

Lawley, James, and Tompkins, Penny, *Metaphors in Mind: Transformation through Symbolic Modelling*, The Developing Company Press, 2011.

Levy, Fran, *Dance/Movement Therapy: A Healing Art*, American Alliance for Health Physical Education and Recreation, 1992.

Linley, Alex, Willars, Janet, and Biswas-Diener, Robert, *The Strengths Book: Be Confident, Be Successful, and Enjoy Better Relationships by Realizing the Best of You*, CAPP Press, 2010.

Lucas, Marsha, *Rewire Your Brain for Love: Creating Vibrant Relationships Using the Science of Mindfulness*, Hay House, 2013.

Maitreya, Ananda, translator, *The Dhammapada*, Parallax Press, 2001.

Martin, Kathleen, Ed., *The Book of Symbols*, Taschen, Germany, 2010.

McDermott, Diane, and Snyder, C.R., *The Great Big Book of Hope*, New Harbinger Publications, 2000.

McDermott, Diane, *Making Hope Happen*, New Harbinger Publications, 1999.

Mehl-Madrona, Lewis, *Healing the Mind through the Power of Story*, Bear and Co., 2010.

Merzenich, Michael, *Soft-Wired: How the New Science of Brain Plasticity Can Change Your Life*, Parnassus Publishing, 2013.

Mikulincer, Mario., and Shaver, Philip, *Attachment in Adulthood*, Guilford Press, 2007.

O'Connor, Richard, *Undoing Perpetual Stress*, Berkley Trade Books, 2006.

Porges, Stephen, *Polyvagal Theory: Neurophysiological Foundations of Emotions, Attachment, Communication, and Self-regulation*, W.W. Norton & Company, 2011.

Ratey, James, *Spark: The Revolutionary New Science of Exercise and the Brain*, Little, Brown, and Co., 2008.

Richo, David, *How to Be an Adult in Relationships: The Five Keys to Mindful Loving*, Shambhala, 2002.

Rosenbery, Stanley, *Accessing the Healing Power of the Vagus Nerve: Self-Help Exercises for Anxiety, Depression, Trauma, and Autism*, North Atlantic Books, 2017.

Salzberg, Sharon, *Loving Kindness: The Revolutionary Art of Happiness*, Shambala, 1995.

Scurlock-Durana, Suzanne, *Full Body Presence: Learning to Listen to Your Body's Wisdom*, New World, 2010.

Somov, Pavel, *Anger Management Jumpstart: A 4-Session Mindfulness Path to Compassion and Change*, PESI Publishing & Media, 2013.

Somov, Pavel, *The Lotus Effect: Shedding Suffering and Rediscovering Your Essential Self*, New Harbinger Publications, 2010.

Sapolsky, Robert, *Why Zebras Don't Get Ulcers*, W.H. Freeman and Co., 1994.

Siegel, Daniel J., and Payne Bryson, Tina, *The Whole Brain Child*, Bantam Books, 2012.

Schwartz, Jeffrey M., and Gladding, Rebecca, *You Are Not Your Brain*, Avery Publishing, 2012.

Schwartz, Jeffrey, and Begley, Sharon, *The Mind and the Brain: Neuroplasticity and the Power of Mental Force*, ReganBooks, 2003.

Schwartz, Jeffrey, *Brain Lock*, Harper Perennial, 1996.

Seligman, Martin, *Learned Optimism*, Vintage Publishers, 2006.

Sheldon, Kennon M., Kashdan, Todd B. and Steger, Michael F., editors, *Designing Positive Psychology*, Oxford University Press, 2011.

Silananda, U., *The Four Foundations of Mindfulness*, Wisdom Publications, 2003.

Snyder, C.R., *The Psychology of Hope*, Free Press, 2003.

Snyder, C.R., *The Handbook of Hope*, Academic Press, 2000.

Snyder, C.R., McDermott, Diane; Cook, William; and Rapoff, Michael A., *Hope for the Journey: Helping Children Through Good Times and Bad*, Westview Press, 1997.

Snyder, C.R., and Ford, C., *Coping with Negative Life Events*, Springer, 1987.

Tarragona, Margarita, *Positive Identities: Narrative Practices and Positive Psychology*, PositiveAcorn. com, 2012.

Tarrant, Jeff, *Meditation Interventions to Rewire the Brain: Integrating Neuroscience Strategies for ADHD, Anxiety, Depression & PTSD*, PESI Publishing & Media, 2017.

Thich Nhat Hanh, *How to Love*, Parallax Press, 2014.

Thich Nhat Hanh, *The Art of Communicating*, HarperOne, 2014.

Thich Nhat Hanh, *Anger: Wisdom for Cooling the Flames*, Riverhead Books, 2002.

van der Kolk, Bessel, *The Body Keeps the Score: Brain, Mind, and Body in the Healing of Trauma*, Penguin Books, 2015.

Whybrow, Peter, *American Mania: When More Is Not Enough*, W.W. Norton & Co., 2006.

WEBSITES

American Dance Therapy Association: **www.adta.org**

Center for Investigating Healthy Minds: **www.centerhealthyminds.org**

Center for Mindful Eating: **www.thecenterformindfuleating.org**

Dana Foundation Brain and Immunology Newsletter: **www.dana.org**

Forgiveness Project: **www.theforgivenessproject.com**

Global Association for Interpersonal Neurobiology Studies: **www.mindgains.org**

Greater Good Science Center: **www.greatergood.berkeley.edu**

Humor Project: **www.humorproject.com**

Laughter Yoga International: **www.laughteryoga.org**

Mind and Life Institute: **www.mindandlife.org**

Mindful Awareness Research Center: **www.marc.ucla.edu**

Mindful Magazine & Website: **www.mindful.org**

Mindfulness Research Monthly: **www.goamra.org**

Network for Grateful Living: **www.gratefulness.org**

Optimist International: **www.optimist.org**